STORYTELLING SKILLS

How To Tell A Good Story And Be Successful In Social Life, Business Communication And Persuasion.

© Copyright 2020 by Fred Hackman

All rights reserved.

This document is geared towards providing exact and reliable information with regard to the topic and issue covered. The publication is sold with the idea that the publisher is not required to render accounting, officially permitted, or otherwise, qualified services. If advice is necessary, legal or professional, a practiced individual in the profession should be bordered.

-From a Declaration of Principles which was accepted and approved equally by a Committee of the American Bar Association and a Committee of Publishers and Associations.

In no way is it legal to reproduce, duplicate, or transmit any part of this document in either electronic means or in printed format. Recording of this publication is strictly prohibited and any storage of this document is not allowed unless with written permission from the publisher. All rights reserved.

The information provided herein is stated to be truthful and consistent, in that any liability, in terms of inattention or otherwise, by any usage or abuse of any policies, processes, or directions contained within is the solitary and utter responsibility of the recipient reader. Under no circumstances will any legal responsibility or blame be held against the publisher for any reparation, damages, or monetary loss due to the information herein, either directly or indirectly.

Respective authors own all copyrights not held by the publisher.

The information herein is offered for informational purposes solely and is universal as so. The presentation of the information is without a contract or any type of guarantee assurance.

The trademarks that are used are without any consent, and the publication of the trademark is without permission or backing by the trademark owner. All trademarks and brands within this

book are for clarifying purposes only and are owned by the owners themselves, not affiliated with this document.

CONTENTS

Introduction 1

Chapter 1: 5w- When, Where, What, Who, Why For Good Storytelling.. 13

Chapter 2: How To Make Your Story Interesting And Believable. 19

Chapter 3: The Power Of Details 29

Chapter 4: Persuasion Techniques 41

Chapter 5: Emphatic Communication 57

Chapter 6: Storytelling In Everyday Social Life 85

Chapter 7: Business Storytelling 89

Conclusion 123

INTRODUCTION

Storytelling is the transmission of events, often by improvisation or embellishment, in words and images.

In every society, stories or myths were exchanged as a means of entertainment, education, cultural preservation, and the instillation of moral values. Crucial elements of storytelling and storytelling include plot, characters, and narrative perspective.

Storytelling has won its position as the most significant practice humans possess. The most important explanation for this is that every tale includes a lesson to teach the audience. Stories encourage us to love, to forgive others, to be just, and to aspire for more than we have. The greatest stories ever told serve as a reflection on the world we live in and on both the goodness and evil present in our culture. The Lord of the Rings offers a great description of the lessons to learn from literature. Through it, we see a world that on the surface greatly differs from our own, a fantastical world of elves and dragons and a quest to conquer evil. As one delves deeper, parallels are apparent between Tolkien's universe and our own; we see his universe represents our own. When reading, we witness a world fraught with conflict and misery, but still decent souls who do their utmost to battle the encroaching darkness. This contrast between what is and what should stand as the main theme of epic sagas. Through this theme, stories create a reflection on our world and demonstrate what must be done to set things right. This shows the importance of stories as teachers. These epic tales are intended to be an example of what can be done to change society and what it means to be human and to make morally correct decisions. Storytelling often fulfills a critical need of society by presenting ideal role models by their characters. It shows average citizens doing exceptional deeds, not because they are compelled to, but because they want to make the right decisions. Their actions prove people can change the world through their daily actions. Throughout history, these role models have driven numerous individuals to excellence Culture owes its knowledge of these amazing role models to the art of telling stories. Storytelling serves as our common way of passing on these epic tales of inspiration. Some of its most important features are its lack of a rigid structure and clear limitations. Each time a story is retold, the person telling it can modify it and change it. It allows a great degree of variation and an ever-changing and developing plot. This fluidity of identity gives storytelling its significance as a tradition and as a medium for teaching. The personalization of the story by the storyteller means that every story, told differently with every recounting, has an endless number of lessons that can be taught. The ability to teach anything and everything in an endless number of ways that can be adapted to the audience makes storytelling the most powerful and significant practice to society today. Storytelling has many significant consequences for our everyday lives. It was one of the most powerful inspirational sources known to man. Storytelling acts as a fantastic teaching tool that imparts life lessons to people of all ages. Storytelling has proved its durability and importance beyond any shadow of a doubt, beginning with the dawn of civilization and continuing in this era of almost immediate access to all knowledge. Its influence has influenced our world in a number of ways, some of which are boringly simple to see and understand, and some of which remain more mysterious and enigmatic in meaning. The value storytelling retains inspiration as a source and, as a teaching method, makes it possess the most important heritage of humanity. Storytelling is about tales. It's about using stories to reach the audience or clarifying something more—naturally, images, videos, and video help to tell a good story too. Stories have also been a form of conveying. They'd tell each other stories before the people knew how to write. It is much easier to recall the stories than plain details. Stories are also entertaining; they stimulate the imagination. That is why parents tell stories to their kids. And we enjoy watching movies and reading books. We enjoy the stories; we are story-addicted.

Using humor in your story will make your story more entertaining-if; you do it the right way. Your story is something that people want to learn about. Stories heighten the audience's interest. When you use stories the right way, stories will help you convey a stronger message. Stories can be of use in making the point. We might be adding clarification. A tale is written to help people understand the value of structuring a clean web. This is a pretty hard topic to understand. A narrative provides meaning. Most importantly, people will remember your story and will remember your post's message, or even your brand, with that. However, if you are using stories in a positive way, you could also encourage people to act. Perhaps you'll encourage people to clean up their website or continue their blog posts and presentations with storytelling.

Storytelling enriches anyone listening's lives, is a perfect form of storytelling, and draws people of all ages. Storytelling often tells the entire history of nations and cultures; the stories are often told with great humor or fire. We are moved through time and space to another dimension by the words and acts of a talented storyteller! The world fades away for a few minutes or hours, and we become a part of something.

There are different reasons to tell stories — selling, entertaining, teaching, or boasting. We'll explore

this below. I want to explore right now why we're choosing storytelling over, say, a data-driven PowerPoint or a bulleted list. Why are stories our way of sharing information, explaining it, and selling it? Here's

the explanation. Stories Solidify Abstract Concepts and Simplify Complex Ideas While attempting to grasp a new concept; we have all encountered uncertainty. Stories give way around that. Think of times when stories helped you to better understand a concept, maybe a teacher used a real-life example to describe a math problem, a preacher explained a situation during a lecture, or a speaker used an example to express complicated knowledge.

Stories help to solidify conceptual abstracts and clarify complex messages. One of the biggest advantages of storytelling in business is taking on a high, non-tangible concept and relating it through concrete ideas. For example, take Apple. Computers and smartphones are a very complicated subject for your average user to identify.

They were able to explain precisely how their goods help consumers using real-life examples instead of relying on technological jargon that very few customers would understand.

Stories Put People Together As I said above, stories are kind of a common language. We all understand the hero story, the underdog story, or the heartbreak tale. We all store emotions and express emotions of elation, hope, frustration, and anger. Sharing in a tale provides a sense of commonality and belonging even among the most diverse people.

Stories put people together in a world separated by a multitude of issues and build a sense of community.

Notwithstanding our language, culture, political preferences, or ethnicity, stories bind us through how we feel and react to them. Stories make us human.

Stories Inspire and Motivate. Stories are making us alive, and so are brands. This brings brands back to earth as they are honest and genuine, which lets customers engage with them and the people behind them.

Tapping into the feelings of people and highlighting the positive as well as the negative is how stories inspire and empower and ultimately push action.

Stories also promote loyalty to the company. Creating a narrative around your brand or business not only humanizes it but also ultimately promotes your business Storytelling can be used in the entertainment, retail, automobile, marketing, e-commerce, and almost all industries. Storytelling can apply to any sector.

In business, search for the core components common to all business-impact stories to identify a true story: Structural: A story has a beginning, middle, and end.

Elementary: A story also has elements that involve a character, a struggle, a journey, a resolution, a shift, and a call for action.

Intrinsic: A story exposes an authentic aspect of the storyteller that elicits emotion in the audience.

Strategic: A plot sparks the imagination of an audience, encourages them to respond to the story's circumstance, and motivates them to take action.

By that description, a business-impact story can be as short as a single paragraph. Or it may be a 3-minute presentation or a 30-minute demonstration of the product. Whatever the case, if it contains the above components strategically, it will have maximum impact.

MAIN ELEMENTS OF STORYTELLING

Below are the five main elements of storytelling.

The Three-Act Formula

Should you fear that the floor will collapse when you visit a shop or restaurant or movie theater and send you falling to the ground below? Do you regularly ask yourself at home if the roof would collapse on you? Let's hope not! Such questions may sound absurd (in more developed countries at least), but I use them to illustrate the significance of the system.

Structure is not only important to a building but to stories as well. If a building's foundation is solid, we are not challenging it. We don't really worry about it, actually, because we don't have to. If something works, we don't even seem to notice it. The same goes for the structure of the plot, which keeps all the elements intact, generally without your knowledge. All strong stories essentially follow the same basic structure: The Theory of the Three-Acts.

Whether it's your favorite book, sitcom, or movie, you can almost always break down the presented story into three parts, or act. In Act, I, the time, place, and setting of the story are directed to you. You meet the main characters, and hopefully, you're fascinated by what's to come next because, at the end of the act, there's a hook (see below). Act I is usually the shortest section of the story since the hook needs to work its magic as soon as possible; otherwise, the tale loses the precious attention of the audience. So Act II reflects the story's principal journey. Typically, this is the longest part of any story, including major and minor failures, understanding moments, profound knowledge, and known and unknown hurdles. Toward the end of Act II, usually, the protagonist faces the main obstacle head-on. We see in Act III how she overcomes that. The main character and her situation have often improved when the issue is resolved, usually for the better. This results in a final, satisfying conclusion and resolution.

As the Three-Act Structure is so significant, let's go over it again below, using as an example the well-known movie The Sound of Music.

We meet principal character(s) in Act I. Gifted songstress and nun-in-training Maria is the lead character in The Sound of Music, and on the eve of the Anschluss in 1938, we first see her singing on a majestic mountaintop in the pre-World War II Alps. Instead, we are met with the hook hopefully by the filmmakers will keep us engaged in the film for its length. As the audience soon learns, the hook is that Maria is not at all confident that she has found the right calling, and we understand that this will be tested when she decides to become the governess for the von Trapp family. The journey ends.

In Act II, things begin to get complicated, and as part of their journey, the main character faces a series of tests/obstacles. In the case of Maria, that means striving to gain the approval of von Trapp's children and, later, the captain's affections, which are already beholden to Baroness Schrader. Maria knows better who she is after several tribulations (hint: not a nun!), but now she and the von Trapps face the challenge of falling into the hands of the Nazis. Usually, this act ends with the question of whether the hero will survive–literally or figuratively–and find a satisfying resolution despite the almost insurmountable odds.

Act III usually addresses all of the story's key questions and takes the main character — and audience— to a satisfactory resolution. In The Sound of Music, in this case, the von Trapps elude the Nazis and goes off into the figurative sunset, or hike into a lovely mountain area. Fading to black. It is love that wins.

The Hook.

The crook.

"Plant a strong hook early in your story to grab the attention of your audience" is easy to tell, but it can be hard to do. And how is it that you build a good hook? Although there are countless potentially relevant hooks, a more structured way to build one is to adopt the "3 Cs "— even if you don't feel especially creative: tension, comparison, and contradiction. I'll describe these instances and then present them. Or put it plainly, a conflict is a collision of powers or desires that go in opposite directions. Yet remember that conflict, such as war or famine, need not be epic. A dispute may be simply about an argument between partners or someone who desperately wants to fall asleep but cannot. Usually, a comparison includes the juxtaposition of two opposite qualities: heavy and light, plentiful and minimal, productive, and apathetic; the list continues. A paradox runs contrary to the viewers' standards. The examples below are the ones my clients wrote from the beginning of the tales. See if you can say if / how each is a conflict, a comparison, or a contradiction.

EXAMPLE 1 "Things began badly on June 21, 2002, with England losing to Brazil in the Football World Cup and getting worse steadily; the fateful day ended with our being finally rescued by the Navy." Circle what you think is the correct answer: Dispute Comparison

CONTRADICTION SAMPLE 2 "I was born and raised in New York. Before I call myself American, I make myself a New Yorker. Yet, a few years ago, my work took me to a small desert village in Sudan. "Circle what you think is the appropriate answer: Dispute Comparison Discrepancy

SAMPLE 3" It was Tuesday at 10:03 a.m., my second day on a new job. Chris, a software developer, explained to me the technologies used by the company. He got an instant message right in the middle of our conversation. He got up quickly and told me,' It's time for a run of the cupcake! Circle if you think the solution is right.

CONFLICT CONTRAST CONTRADICTION

Let's talk about it now. Essentially, Example 1 is a classic dispute. Actually, in this beginning, there are two stages of conflict to a much longer story. Firstly, one team opposes the other in any competitive team sport. All teams want to be triumphant, but only one is. Yet the opening means a second fight, too. The last thing that comes to mind when you're well and safe is having to get someone to rescue you, particularly not the Navy! So, the concept of a confrontation between the need to live and a life-threatening event or force is rooted in this story. And most listeners will say, "The storyteller must want some kind of trouble so that the Navy will need to intervene? "Some customers also say that this connection also represents a contradiction: Why would someone watching the World Cup, suddenly find their lives in danger and need the Navy? This hook may, in reality, be a fallacy, too. Every hook can be one of 3 C's or more!

Exhibit 2 is the opposite. Also, if you've never been to New York City or Sudan, the major difference between a bustling metropolis and a desolate, sparsely populated desert village can be easily imagined. The contrast is potent and immediate.

Best presented as a paradox is Example 3. One doesn't leave a conversation with a new colleague in most work settings too suddenly just to go buy desserts!

Regardless of the precise form of hook that is portrayed, all three examples make us wonder exactly what is happening in the plot, and make us want to learn more. Your hook will do just that: get your viewers excited and ready to learn more.

Challenge and Change

"Super optimistic people with no issues and perfect relationships and perfect parenting are not good entertainment," said Matthew Weiner, producer of the hit television show Mad Men. Weiner, like any great television, movie, or advertisement maker, recognizes that obstacles build excitement, which in effect motivates sustained media attention. This also induces tension in the main characters, in their circumstances, or (ideally) both, to have a central challenge in your plot. If the challenge is a story's nerve center, then the shift is its soul. When anything or all at the end of the tale stays the same, then what is the point of the journey? Innately, people want to know not only what happened in the narrative, but what's different at the end and why.

A Clear Theme

How do you normally say when you're asked to introduce yourself to a panel discussion or similar event? Most likely, the presentation follows a simple chronological order full of facts (where you come from, academic qualifications, job history). Unfortunately, recounting incidents or achievements is not the same as telling a story, no matter how good they may be. A story needs to have a thread, and chronology isn't enough. To order for audiences to understand and appreciate the theme of the story, the storyteller needs to tell his stories by bringing together events and reflection.

CHAPTER 1: 5W– WHEN, WHERE, WHAT, WHO, WHY FOR GOOD STORYTELLING

One of the best practices for authors is to follow the rules of "The 5Ws" by exploring a story's Who, What, Where, When, and Why.

When you can't find out what makes your story special and interesting, then chances are that no one else can.

<u>WHEN</u>

During what time (day, day, month, year)? When was the most recent update? If you would expect to know more, when? How will the results become felt?

How did the story happen, or when would the incident occur?

Too much, I see a wonderful article about an upcoming conference or event, and the writer doesn't mention the date or time once in the post. Pay attention to this information, and your stories will stand out as well as thoroughly written writing pieces.

- Which date is it?

• Which time is it?

• At the same time, what happens? Is it a focused season? Is the weather it's ideal then for this event?

WHERE

Where is this happening (building, neighborhood, state, country)? Where will readers go to find out more?

How did this story happen, or where will it happen?

Look right into here. Since you cover a venue, you're going to want to go into as much detail as you can possibly. Show the listener, rather than just telling them. For example, rather than writing that it was a hot day, write that the person's hair stuck from the sweat trickling down from her scalp to the back of her neck. Let the reader think the hot and humid air came in. You'll drag her into your article if you can show the reader, and hold her there.

• What's the place like?

• What do you call it?

• Are there, odors?

• What sounds are they?

• Are there any little known information about this location that the reader might find interesting?

WHAT

What has happened? What are the Impacts? For the listener, what does that mean?

It should have a central message if the story is one page or twenty, ten minutes, or sixty. It needs to be set up like the base of a home before going forward.

Does your story sell a product, or raise money? Explaining a program or campaigning for a specific issue? What's the point of that story? Try summing up the story in six to ten words to better describe this. You don't have a central message when you can't do that.

What's an important part of the story as it shows you what happened to the case or action? The robbery is the" what"' of the story is a tale of a woman being robbed by an anonymous male. The" what" can be an occurrence, moment, or something that could be described as occurring. They may also apply to any items, records, literature, musical works, or other aspects of the overall story that are essential information.

It is a perfect method of thinking that holds the boundaries of the audience in mind. We rarely recall whole stories; more often than not, it's brief quotations, scenes, characters, or ideas.

And put yourself in the listener's shoes in her car or walk with earbuds down the lane. She has just put the story to a close. What do you think of her? Did she leave to ponder a question? A new way to see your neighborhood, your city, or your country?

You should create your stories to have the effect that you want them to have — bearing in mind what you want the viewer to remember when you read, compose, and produce. (Yes, you should always be able to pivot when you know new stuff in your reporting.)

WHO

Who drives the story? Who are they? How will you be affected? Who does benefit from this? Why is it that loses? Who might like to hear your story? Who will profit the most, and who will respond?

Who determines the subject being debated, or persons? It is the person that the author is talking about in a news article. It may also involve offenders, suspects, and everyone else who is an important part of the investigation. This can be regarded as the principal character in terms of other fiction. You need to consider your audience and who will react and take action to construct a compelling tale.

Do some research on your target market and identify your customer persona(s) before you put pen to paper (or cursor to a word processor). This method will familiarize you with who might read, view, or listen to your story. When you build the base of your plot, it will also provide critical guidance for the next few steps.

WHY

Why was the thing happening? What on the big picture is this important? Why is it that readers will care?

A short path to real human interaction and influence: Have you addressed after-the-fact with a presenter and said, "I don't know. I just didn't get in touch with them? If so, you understand firsthand how important it is to communicate with your audience to create a living, breathing. While strong presentation skills are going a long way towards creating that link, storytelling can be the thing that puts the presentation above all else.

Why? For what? In a business environment, when you say a story, you personalize the facts and add a human face to the information that you're presenting. Ultimately the data relates to real people in the real world, and the audience gets a glimpse into how the content has influenced you, the speaker.

A refreshing breath of air for data-heavy information: Sometimes, we need to move away from the situation and think about it in another light, or after a while, to analyze a big idea more thoroughly. Telling a story during a talk gives the audience the chance to do just that. It's the pause that refreshes and helps them to come back with a new perspective to your content, post-story.

CHAPTER 2: HOW TO MAKE YOUR STORY INTERESTING AND BELIEVABLE.

1. YOUR OPENING MUST CREATE QUESTIONS IN THE MIND OF YOUR AUDIENCE

If you generate questions in the minds of your audience, you have them hooked into your story because you have created curiosity about them. Look at the opening of your Story and ask yourself, "What questions will pop up in the minds of my viewers as soon as I offer this opening? "If there are no questions for your audience... you need a new opening.

2. INTRODUCE SOON, THE PROBLEM / CONFLICT ON WHAT MAKES US PLUG INTO CERTAIN STORIES?

How do certain stories place us at the edge of our seats? What mysterious elements captivate in a story?

You have to grasp this next idea if you want to learn how to keep the listeners interested in your presentation.

Conflict is the number one thing that makes a story compelling-that has the audience sitting on the edge of their seats in anticipation, totally captivated by your every word.

What is meant by conflict?

Conflict means to fight. It is a war between the powers that oppose it. A war of life and death. A war of hate and forgiveness. A war between liberty and oppression. As long as there are two solid, opposing forces that make the story's outcome uncertain, a story will grip you. It holds our enterprise. This makes us uncomfortable. It makes us wonder, "What's going to happen next? "It's not a really interesting story with no tension. There is no mystery and no tension when there's no dispute. There's no "What's next? "Issue. We already know what is coming next, without confrontation. We're not interested, and we don't get involved as a result.

Let me send you a stunning example. Titanic, the blockbuster movie, is a perfect movie because it involves so many conflicts. Life and death dispute is the first and most visible. When the Titanic sinks, we wonder, "Do they live or die? "In addition, many of the movie's exciting scenes involve minor conflicts. For starters, we find out there aren't enough lifeboats on the ship during one scene, so the dispute becomes "Who does and who doesn't get into the lifeboat? "The second big conflict in the film is whether Jack and Rose, the two main characters, can manage to remain together or not. Will love prevail, or will they be divided by society because they come from radically different backgrounds?

Titanic wouldn't be such a great movie, without all the tension. After all, not many people would pay for watching Titanic if only the two characters met on a ship, fell heads over heels in love, and lived happily afterward. Yeah, we'd like to believe we'd be interested in a story without tension because it wouldn't bring us through emotional stress, but the shocking fact is that the plot tension is what keeps members of the audience watching a film. It's also what's going to keep your viewers informed on your show.

First, introduce the dispute early in the speeches and presentations. The confrontation catches the interest of the viewer as it has the members of the audience, thinking, "I wonder how this will end."

3. PROVIDE SENSORY INFORMATION TO BREATHE LIFE INTO YOUR CHARACTERS

If you've ever had a fantastic speech, you know it's more than what the speaker has said. It's about the mental picture created for you by the speaker, too. Engaging a public is more than simply giving valuable information.

Executive Story coach Patricia Fripp says, "People don't remember what you're saying as much as they remember what they're seeing when you're saying it." That means your speeches need to help the audience get an understanding and build a visual picture.

Only think about the last great novel you've read. A visual image was generated by the words on the screen. You could see the characters in your mind and see their actions. The same must be done with a fantastic Narrative.

One of my favorite examples of this in speaking is from TED chat, Choice, Joy, and Spaghetti Sauce by Malcom Gladwell. He defines a character named Howard in it by saying: "Howard's about that big, and he's round, and he's in his sixties. He has big giant glasses and thinning grey hair, and a kind of wonderful exuberance and vitality. He has a parrot, and enjoys the opera, and is a great medieval history aficionado. He's a psychophysicist by profession. "see when you say it." That means the speeches ought to help the audience get an understanding and create a visual picture.

Only think about the last great novel you've read. A visual image was generated by the words on the screen. You could see the characters in your mind and see their actions. The same must be done by a fantastic narrative.

• It is important to keep your characters alive by providing details of how they look.

• You always want to give your audience sensory details that help them to develop a mental image of your characters

• Always follow the principle of "show" instead of "tell."

4. CREATE VISUAL MOTION PICTURES FOR YOUR VIEWERS USING ALL OF YOUR SENSES.

Through creating explanations that use as many of those senses as possible, you can help the audience build an image of your characters and stories in mental motion.

The real strength of a story is that it offers a wealth of sensory knowledge for the viewer to make it come alive. You can imagine what's going on within your mind's eye, like a motion picture.

Having one or more of the five senses in your conversations will help you do so. Those senses include:

- Visual (sight)

- Auditory (sound)

- Kinaesthetic (touch, emotions)

- Olfactory (smell)

- Visual Gustatory (taste)

Visual–What do you see in that short story? Could you imagine the knife and the man with his "large thumb and well-calloused forefinger" holding the sheep scrotum?

Auditory-What sounds do you hear? It's the ripping sound of "Velcro being yanked off a sticky board" that stands out to me.

Kinaesthetic–How do you feel? There were references to the sheep's scrotum being "firmly held." And maybe you've even gone to a point where you can feel the sheep's pain.

Storytelling Skills | 23

Olfactory-What are you going to smell? This passage does not apply to any specific smells, but if this is something you're familiar with, you may start to imagine the scent of livestock on a farm.

Gustatory–You could taste what? Again, there is no clear taste definition, but it may have left a bad taste in your mouth!

5. INCLUDE DETAILED DETAILS

It's important to note when writing your personal story that you need to provide as many detailed details as possible. To turn your story into a mental film for your audience, provide as many precise details as possible for the audience members. Of example, instead of saying, "The man was huge," say, "He was about 6 foot 5 inches." Instead of saying, "I spoke to a large group of people," say, "I spoke to a group of 500 CEOs." Do you see how the specifics help you see the scene? Non-specific comments like "the man was tall" don't help members of your audience imagine the characters and the scene in their head. Saying, "He was roughly 6 foot 5, with muscular muscles," gives the viewers enough detail to be able to visualize the characters and the scene. Use non-specific language when writing your plot. Provide the characters, scenes, and dates with specific details. The specific details will help the audience see what you're doing, as well as add your presentation to internal credibility.

BOTTOMLINE:

• Clear detail lets the audience understand what you mean.

- Specificity adds to the presentation of internal credibility.

- Include precise character descriptions, scenes, and dates at all times.

6. SEARCH FOR HUMOR OPPORTUNITIES INSIDE DIALOG

The best stories at the same time, get the members of the audience to laugh and understand.

Humour doesn't mean the Internet needs to steal jokes. For many reasons, I advise against using Internet jokes:

- Internet jokes are typically not funny.

- Funny ones are typically well known. The joke is likely to be known to your audience members, ensuring they know the punch line. If they are aware of the punch line, the joke loses the element of suspense (the abrupt twist) and will thus not yield a laugh.

- Jokes understate your reputation. If members of the audience have heard the joke before, then they will mark you as unoriginal. The negative view is going to be difficult to overcome.

- Jokes seem to diminish your message. Generally, they don't have to do with your story and take away your key message. Members of the audience dislike hearing jokes which have nothing to do with the voice.

So, if you don't want to use jokes, how do you add humor to your Story?

Look for space for laughter inside the dialogue.

If you have an exchange of character dialogue, look for openings for humor. What kind of witty comment might a character make? Which kind of humorous dialog line would you add?

Let's look at examples of dialog comedy in I went to the receptionist and said, "Excuse me, are you validating? She looked up and said,' Yes, I do, you have a beautiful smile.' (Laughter of the audience) Now, here's the secret to humor: a joke is funny when it sets the expectation, and then it falls.

The line ("Excuse me, do you validate?") sets the assumption that a "Yes" or a "No" will be the next response, but the line of the receptionist ("Well, yes I do, you have a beautiful smile") breaks the illusion and thus causes the audience members to laugh.

This is also a fantastic wordplay. There are two definitions of the term validate. The first interpretation is that a parking ticket is "authenticated." The second sense is about helping people to feel good about themselves. Lance's line refers to the first sense (about parking), setting the assumption that the answer from the receptionist will be about the ticket for parking. But, by referring to the second interpretation, the answer to the receptionist breaks the assumption. Could wordplay be used to add charm to your speeches?

7. RESOLUTION

There should be a resolution to the dispute in any story. Through this address, the conclusion is that as soon as Lance starts to support the people around him, his life gets better: I went to see my mother–"And I thanked her for taking so much care of me that she needed me to be as nice as I could be." I went to work, and I appreciated my boss for hiring me, he did me a favor, and I started to enjoy my job even more. "Chi chink" What's in your story about settling the conflict?

8.THE SPARK, THE CHANGE, AND TAKEAWAY

We know that it's what makes the tension in a story exciting. And we also know that what inspires viewers is positive-message stories.

Between the conflict and the character's final victory, we have what I call the "spark." The spark refers to the method, idea, or insight, which helps the character to resolve the conflict.

The spark is among the story's most important pieces. It's the method or knowledge that members of the audience will take home with them and use in their own lives to resolve conflict.

The Spark: The spark is the insight or the mechanism the hero gets in your story to resolve the conflict.

The Transition: As a result of the dispute, the characters must transition. The character must vary-either the circumstances of the situation or his / her attitude-as he/she has resolved the conflict.

The Takeaway: There must be one key takeaway message in each story. "Tell a lie, make a case," said Bill Gove, the first president of the National Speakers Association. What's your key takeaway message?

Summarize the main message in a simple, concise sentence to remember and repeat it to the audience.

CHAPTER 3: THE POWER OF DETAILS

A fictional work must be produced, as it were, by brushstroke. The writer may have a vision of the big picture, but nothing really works, especially a plot, if there are not the tiny, vivid, authenticating details. Tiny, specific details seem to be the difference between a working story and a bad story, between a decent piece of fiction writing and a great piece of fiction writing.

As a novel, you should consider stuff like the books on a bookcase for a character, the paintings on his walls, the colors of his walls, the kind of vehicle he drives, the kinds of outfits he wears, his preferences in food, music, movies, friends, wines. You don't really have to have a lot of details. Of course, you don't want free information that just annoys your reader. Again, the background is everything. In certain stories, it may not be appropriate to explain the looks of the main character at all, or to talk about what kind of vehicle he drives or the city in which he lives, as these aspects may not be important to that particular story, but of course, there will be something else. For example, there is no explanation of the characters in Ernest Hemingway's "Hills Like White Elephants." It doesn't matter how they look. What are they doing? And they're effectively evoking their emotions through their dialogue. To know what the characters are like wouldn't add to the plot. Their physical appearances are simply not significant; they are not part of the problems they deal with or the emotions they experience.

You want to avoid details that do not add to the intellectual and emotional enjoyment of the reader, but more often than not, fiction is poor, not due to gratuitous details but due to the lack of accurate, sensual details. Your reader can see, hear, sound, taste, and even smell the world you are building in fiction. So only with clear, sensual information can you activate the reader's senses.

Take chances. Avoid flat, merely authenticating facts without which the story might be better off, but don't be afraid with any emotional charge of the detail. Writers may also ruin an early draft of a story out of their fear of being sentimental, by stripping it of the information that gave it vitality. If you are moved by detail as you write a story, there is a possibility that the reader may be moved as well. When you are afraid of being labeled sentimental, or of exposing something about yourself, you risk never being poignant and committing the greatest sin— the one fatal sin a writer can commit: being boring.

It's usually the tiny information that will not only add immediacy but also originality to your writing. If you write sincerely about the way you see life, about your characters and the circumstances in which they find themselves and the implications and consequences of those circumstances, and if you write beautifully, activate the senses of your reader and make him feel genuinely part of your world of fiction, then the originality will exist in your writing. It will mainly happen because you are a special human being. No one in the world will ever imagine, view, or tell the very same story.

The story's idea of "the big picture" may not be much of anything new. Take the first Rocky movie, for example, the 1976 Academy Award winner for the best picture. There's a lot about Rocky's idea that would strike many as trite: a down-and-out fighter named Rocky gets a shot at the title. None of that is really original. But what makes the film succeed is that the characters come to life, and they are recognizable to the viewer and interested in them. Small specifics like the pet turtles of Rocky, the photos on his walls, the void in his tee-shirt, the words he uses habitually –all these little things play a huge part in his growth of character. (The same would, of course, be right if Rocky were a short story or book or memoir.) By the way, the sequels to Rocky do not work as well as the emphasis is not so much on the people and the small details as it is on training scenes and battle scenes and melodramatic arguments between the characters— the sensational rather than the human elements.

The topic of a story is almost always people, whatever else the story may be concerned with, and originality comes not so much from the subject matter as from the subject's care. You don't have to look for anything crazy to write about — as a professional bigamist wrestler (although the story might be fine). You might write about anything that sounds boring when summarized — for example, an old lady who lives alone in a wooded cottage and does nothing but work in her yard with flowers and drink tea before going to bed at night.

It all comes down to the minute details. The old lady, her home, her flowers and the scent and taste of her tea, as well as the feeling of the smooth, porcelain cup in her hand, become very real for the reader in the hands of a good writer, and the tale ends up being very convincing.

Stories based on significant or fascinating themes that are accompanied by small yet revealing details are more full as they offer more to the reader to catch.

Observation is the key to accuracy.

Writer Michael Connelly had been a police reporter at the South Florida Sun-Sentinel and Los Angeles Times until he became a best-selling crime writer.

Throughout his 2004 novel, Crime Beat, Connelly mentions spending a week watching a murder squad and witnessing "the single most important thing I've ever seen as a crime writer." Connelly witnessed the detective removing his glasses to rub his eyes on the final day as he sat in the squad supervisor's office, going over last-minute details before returning to the newspaper to compose his article.

"As he dropped the glasses on his desk," Connelly says, "I found there was a deep groove cut into the earpiece. It was like locating a diamond in the desert, for I knew exactly how the groove got there. "He had seen the sergeant approach the victim's body in murder scenes, and take off his glasses, hooking them in his mouth at all times.

"I realized that his teeth clenched so tightly on them as he stuck his glasses in his mouth, that they were cut into the rough earpiece plastic. Something about the man, the work, the universe, it said. It was a telling detail that opened a window into the life of that guy. It said all that needed to be said about his commitment, encouragement, and relationship to his work. "Connelly says he instinctively knew that whether it was a newspaper crime story or a detective novel," My life as a writer had to be about following the narrating information. "Using specifics in a story is similar to providing other facts. A good story is based not just on facts, but on "the right facts," details that shed light on "the truth about the facts." Good stories represent good choices or, as Scott Libin, former news director and faculty member of Poynter, says, "selection instead of compression."

HOW TO GIVE DETAILS IN A STORY.

Creating information into your story is an ability many authors are struggling to master. Always quoted, but not always understood, is the old adage "show don't say" Details help you create or display everything from the setting of your story to descriptions of characters to feelings of a character. You need acute observational skills and sensitivity to all five of the senses to produce unique and concise descriptions. When you include in your writing descriptions of sight, sound, touch, smell, and taste, you're well on your way to crafting a story full of good descriptions.

Keep a notebook always with you to capture fascinating and unusual details that occur in your everyday life. You do not know whether or not any observation will end up as a detail of your story, but keeping a summary notebook will help you practice the art of examining your surroundings for potential details of the story. Document how a woman wears her hair in a particular style in the grocery store, or the odd gait of an elderly person traversing the street. All this information might be useful while you're writing.

Work with five senses. Stories should contain information that focuses on all five senses. For example, when you describe a character, you should include information about his cologne scent and the sound that he makes when he laughs. For any piece of detail, you don't need to use all five senses but push yourself to incorporate all the senses into a complete tale. Writers sometimes forget about smell and sound, because all day long you're surrounded by odors and noises. Know your characters are living in a world full of sounds and odors. To create a more descriptive atmosphere, integrate certain senses into your plot.

Avoid telling a reader how he feels like a character. Instead of writing that a character is frustrated, demonstrate how she gets her fists clenched and stomps her feet. Your reader can understand how upset the character is with the specifics you use to portray her personality. For certain instances writing detailed descriptions allows you to slow down as you compose and spend ample time imagining all the elements of a particular scene that will make it come to life for the reader.

Using metaphor to equate elements of your story to photos that might seem unrelated but still invoke the reader's connections. For example, the ash that flies away from a fire could be contrasted with white butterflies that escape the flames. Imagining ash as white butterflies bring a unique insight to the reader that catches his imagination and improves his reading of your novel.

TIP: Choose story information which is important for the development of the plot or character. Especially when writing a short story, every detail has to contribute to the overall story. If you spend a few sentences explaining how a character on Tuesdays often wears a certain sweater, that information must be important to the larger plot of the tale.

Using clear descriptions in your writing differentiates between vocabulary that springs to life and words that stay flat and uninspiring.

Wherever in your novel, you use specifics–and particularly in the passages of descriptive writing–always seek to find a deeper, more interesting, more compelling description.

Why are they so big?

All novels are elaborate lies–authors know that and readers know that. The unspoken idea is that authors should seek to make their stories as life-like as possible so that readers will at least believe that what they are really reading is happening.

And the way writers do this is, primarily, by using solid, concrete, authentic details.

Below are three things to remember.

1. Using The Best Specifics

You can imagine sitting down to think about the right specifics would most definitely be commonplace those that come to mind easily. It is not healthy for you. To find accurate, original, and fascinating specifics to use in your writing, you have to search harder. In other words,

• Do not characterize the eyes of a waitress as blue-tell. They are as blue as the neon in the flashing sign outside the Grill of Frankie.

• Don't smoke fat cigars with a businessman–let him smoke Montecristo No. 2s.

• Don't characterize the boy as obsessively in love with the prettiest girl in class–show him scraping her initials with a pencil sharpener blade into his forearm.

Also, try to find unique or unpredictable ways to explain it. For example, if you're describing an approaching storm, you might mention the angry clouds or the wind that bends the trees–the obvious details that everyone uses. But a stronger piece of descriptive writing might concentrate on the fearsome reaction of the character's horse to the storm.

2. Don't Use Too Many Specifics.

It is the consistency that counts, not quantity, in the descriptive prose. Yeah, you have to work hard to find certain unique, original, fascinating information in your fiction to use. Have faith in them once you have it. Do not feel the need to back them up with a dozen needless information.

Here's why it's a bad idea to overuse information in your writing. Part of the fun of reading books is that it helps us to use our imagination. For example, if I imagine the world's most beautiful woman, it would definitely be a very different image than the one in your mind's eye.

When we see a character portrayed on a television screen as the most beautiful woman in the world, we are compelled to share the same picture (and the woman may not be quite that attractive to one or both of us).

But each time we imagine a new image in our heads, the two women will be beautiful to us when we read a novel.

So here's the thing. If I use only two or three striking details to explain the physical appearance of a fictional character, you, the reader, are free to paint the rest of the picture for yourself.

But if I explain this person's every possible physical feature, I'll have done all the research for you and deprived you of the ability to build a picture more to your taste.

Let's go back to the waitress working at Frankie's Grill I described earlier, to explain that. I have already told you her eyes in the flashing sign are as blue as the neon. Here are a few more specifics regarding her appearance.

• At the end of a nine-hour shift, she looks as new as she did at the beginning.

• Just one of her smiles is all it takes for the boys to want to get married to her and the older people to want to be young again.

And this is all about this fictional character that I want to say. You are free to paint yourself the rest of the picture. You can make her blonde or a redhead, short or tall–it's your duty.

That is the read fiction magic!

Precisely the same thing applies to portraying characters by their acts. When a character is abusive, say, by making him kick the dog as he comes into the house, you might demonstrate that. (Okay, maybe dog-kicking isn't especially new and fascinating as writing specifics go, but it's going to happen for now.) The dog incident reveals that he's a perfectly good aggressive guy–there's no need to make him hit his mom, chuck the TV out the window and punch a hole in the wall when his spaghetti's cold.

There will, of course, be more crime to come before the story is done.

And because you were restrained early on and did not use too many specifics in the novel's early stages, when it comes, the violence would be all the more surprising.

What about using minimal detail to explain the settings?

You do it exactly the same way –just use two or three vibrant brush strokes to build the rest of the atmosphere and leave it to the reader. So, for example, if you're describing a spooky cottage.

• Start with an overall impression-a huge, isolated cottage being choked by ivy.

• Provide even more detailed information as the character goes inside and walks about–the breeze-swinging cobwebs, the warm air-chill, the broken staircase.

• Just don't take it too far. Provide just a few telling details, and most of the images will be produced by the readers themselves.

3. Some Specifics Are Easier If They "Fly"

I have spoken about writing being like painting an image in this whole section on definition. I said that fiction is not a visual medium but that it can still allow its readers "see" through the skillful use of language authors.

But it is not a perfect comparison to painting an image.

Pictures are static and unmoving, which is good for photographers and musicians, but not so perfect for storytellers. It's a good start for us to paint pictures for readers, but those pictures would be all the more important if they have the added dimension of motion.

Look at this definition of a house in a novel. "Oak Tree Cottage has been uninhabited for over a decade now. The once-white walls had turned the same muddy green as the front pond, and the paint around the windows had either flaked, or the wind had already taken hold of it. Some of the terracotta roof tiles have also been missing–probably shattered on the bricks below, but in the leaves of last season, it was difficult to tell with the route ankle-deep."

Compare it now with this definition, which shifts a little. "Oak Tree Cottage had been uninhabited for over a decade now. The once-white walls had turned the same dirty green as the front pond, and the paint hanging around the windows that hadn't already gone was hanging in flakes that drifted in this way and that in the wind. Many of the terracotta roof tiles have also been missing–probably shattered on the bricks below, but in the swirling leaves of last season, it was difficult to tell with the path ankle-deep."

Nice, right?

Note that with the first explanation, there is something particularly wrong. Static descriptive writing in a novel can still be vibrant and will catch the attention of the reader.

Nevertheless, displaying information in motion can really make a "word picture" come to life.

CHAPTER 4: PERSUASION TECHNIQUES

Why are certain persons so incredibly persuasive? Could we all use those skills? Here are the 21 crucial lessons I have established to convince people after researching the most prominent political, financial, business, and religious figures, and having tried countless methods out myself. This is a summary from a talk I've been giving to thousands of entrepreneurs on "How to Convince People" for many years now. More detailed examples are discussed in the links below.

THE BASICS

1. Persuasion is not Bribery

Manipulation is intimidation by force to get others to do something they are not interested in doing. Persuasion is the art of getting people to do things that favor you, too, in their own best interest.

2. Persuade the Persuadable

In view of the right timing and meaning, each may be convinced, but not usually in the short term. Election campaigns depend on a select group of swing voters who decide on elections. The first step in persuasion is always to recognize those people who are persuasive to your point of view at a given time, and to concentrate your energies and attention on them.

3. Context and Timing

Context and timing are fundamental building blocks of persuasion. Context provides a general norm for what is appropriate. The Stanford Prisoner Experiment, for example, showed that overachieving students could be transformed into dictatorial prison guards. Timing determines what we want out of life and from others. We have decided to marry a different type of person than when we are younger because we want to change what we want.

4. You must be interested in being convinced

you will never convince someone who is not interested in what you think. Each of us is most interested in ourselves and spend much of our time thinking either about money, love or health. The first art of persuasion is to learn how to communicate about them regularly with people; if you do that, then you will still have their captive attention.

5. Reciprocity Compels

You feel obligated to do something for me because I do something for you. It's part of our evolutionary History to help one another out to live as a species. Most specifically, you will systematically exploit reciprocity in your favor. By offering other people little tokens of consideration, you will ask for more back in return, which others can gladly provide. (TIP:

read Robert Cialdini's "Influence")6. Persistence Pays-Eventually the most persuasive is the individual who is able to keep asking for what they want and continues to display interest. Ultimately, the reason that so many historical figures have influenced millions of people is by remaining constant in their actions and message. Consider Abraham Lincoln, who lost his parents, three daughters, a niece, his girlfriend, struggled in business, and lost eight different elections before being elected US President.

7. Compliment Genuinely

Compliments affect us all so strongly, and we're more likely to trust people we feel good for. Seek to genuinely and always praise others for something they are not usually complimented for; it's the best thing you can do to impress someone that costs nothing but a moment of thought.

8. Set Expectations

A great deal of persuasion is controlling the desires of others to believe in your judgment. The CEO who promises to increase revenue by 20 percent and delivers a 30 percent rise is praised while the same CEO who promises to rise by 40 percent and delivers 35 percent is punished. Persuasion is simply about knowing and overstretching the perceptions of others.

9. Don't Presume

Don't ever presume what someone wants, give your interest always. In sales, we will always refrain from selling our products/services because we believe that others have little money or interest. Don't presume what others will or may not want, give what you can provide and leave them with the decision.

10. Create Scarcity

In addition to the essentials of life, virtually all have relative value. We want things because those things are what other people want. If you want anyone to want what you have, you've got to make the item scarce, even if it's yourself.

11. Creating Urgency

You have to be able to instill in people a sense of urgency to want to act immediately. When we are not driven enough right now to do anything, it is unlikely we can find any motivation in the future. In the present, we have to convince people, and our most important card to play is urgency.

12. Images Matter

What we see is more important than what we listen to. That could be why pharmaceutical firms are now so open about their medications' potentially horrific side effects, even set against a backdrop of people enjoying a sunset in Hawaii. Consider your first impressions fine. Then master the ability to create a picture of a potential experience you will have for others in their mind's eye.

13. Truth

Just by telling them the things about themselves that no one else is able to reveal, the most powerful way to convince others. The most painful, important things that arise in our lives are to face hard truths. Truth-tell without prejudice or bias, and you will also hear very unexpected responses from others.

14.14. Building Report

We like people like us. It extends to our unconscious attitudes beyond our deliberate decisions. By mirroring and matching certain common behaviors (the language of the body, cadence, voice patterns, etc.), you will create a sense of connection where people feel more relaxed with you and are more open to suggestions.

15. Personal Skills.

Behavioural Versatility-Who's in charge is the person with the most versatility, not necessarily the most influence. Kids are also so convincing as they are able to go through a litany of actions to get what they want (putting, screaming, negotiating, begging, charming), while parents are left with the simple "No" answer. The greater the behavioral arsenal, the more convincing you are going to be.

16. Learn Energy Transfer

Some people drain our energy from us, while others are infusing us with it. The most convincing people know how to move their resources, inspire and invigorate them to others. Often it's as simple as eye contact, physical touch, laughter, or even active listening in verbal responses.

17. Clearly, Communicating Is Important

If you are unable to explain your idea or point of view to an 8th grader, so that they can explain it to another adult with adequate clarification, it is too difficult. The art of persuasion is to simplify everything down to its heart and express what they really care about to others.

18. Being Prepared Gives You The Advantage

It will always be your starting point to learn more about the people and the circumstances around you. Preparation meticulously allows for successful persuasion. For example, in a job interview, you significantly increase the chances, becoming well versed in the goods, services, and history of the business.

19. Detach and Stay Calm in Confrontation

No one is more successful when they're "On Tilt." You'll still have the most control in circumstances of heightened tension by staying cool, relaxed, and unemotional. In a confrontation, people turn to those who control their feelings and trust them to guide them in those moments.

20. Using Rage Deliberately

Confrontation is painful for most people. When you're able to escalate a situation to a higher degree of stress and confrontation, certain people would, in certain cases, go back down. Do this sparingly, and do not do so from an emotional position or because of a lack of self-control. But note, for your benefit, you can use rage intentionally.

21. Trust and Certainty

No consistency is as persuasive, intoxicating, and appealing as certainty. It is the person who has an unbridled sense of certitude that can often convince others. If you really believe in what you do, you will always be able to convince others to do what is best for them, and at the same time getting what you want back.

THE PSYCHOLOGICAL THEORIES OF INFLUENCE AND PERSUASION

One of my favorite sites to read about psychological theories is the Dave Straker's Changing Minds website, full of theories written in layman's terms, easily grouped into clear categories and groups for easy reference purposes. One such group is persuasion and Straker lists dealing with how to persuade others.

Here's a quick rundown of each of the ten hypotheses, all of which may sound familiar to you— because you've used them in the past, or because you've had someone using them on you. To read more about all of these, click through the links to see the studies and examples cited by Changing Minds.

1. Amplification Hypothesis The mentality hardens when you convey a specific mentality with certainty. The reverse is also true: the mindset is relaxed by voicing confusion.

2. Theory of conversion The minority in a group may exert a disproportionate impact on those in the majority. Usually, those most vulnerable in the majority are those who could have entered because it was easy to do so, or who thought like there were no

alternatives. The most powerful of these are strong, positive minority voices.

3. Information manipulation theory This theory involves one of the four conversational maxims being intentionally violated by a convincing person. Here are the four: • Quantity: Complete and complete detail.

• Quality: The honest and correct details.

• Relation: Conversational knowledge is important.

• Manner: Data is readily understood, and non-verbal acts reflect the tone of the declaration

4. Priming

You can be affected by factors that affect how you interpret thoughts and behaviors in the short run. Here's a very clever example from Changing Minds: A stage magician in different sentences says' seek' and' loop' in priming a person to think about the word ' loop' later.

5. Reciprocity principle

A universal social principle, reciprocity entails our duty to return favors that others have done.

6. Scarcity Theory

You want a short supply of what's. This drive rises when you expect the disappointment you may have in failing to act quickly enough.

7. Sleeper Effect

Persuasive messages appear to diminish in persuasiveness over time, with the exception of messages from outlets with low credibility. Messages that start with low persuasion are gaining traction as our minds gradually disassociate the source from the content (i.e., a potentially sleazy car salesman and his advice on what car is best).

8. Social influence

Others profoundly influence us based on how we view our relationship with the influencer. Social evidence on-site copying, for example, is convincing if the testimonials and feedback come from reputable outlets, major brands, or peers.

9. Yale Attitude Change Approach

This approach, based on Yale University's many years of study, has identified a variety of factors in persuasive speech, including being a confident, attractive speaker, when first or last is important, and the ideal demographics to target.

10. 10. Ultimate Words Some terms bear more strength than others. This theory splits convincing words into three categories: the language of God: those words which carry blessings or require obedience/sacrifice. For example, advancement, value Devil words: words that are hated, and that evoke disgust. For example, charismatic terms authoritarian, pedophile: those terms that are intangible, less measurable than either God or Devil. For example, equality, contribution These ten theories could be considered as the building blocks for the persuasive

techniques discussed below. Having this psychological base in place, let us move on to other applications of these ideas in your social media marketing, website design, and content development.

HOW TO WRITE About WHAT WE ALL DESIRE

We all know how important survival is to food, water, shelter, and warmth. Some thoughts on what's most important next?

The Needs Hierarchy pyramid, suggested in the 1940s by psychologist Abraham Maslow, reveals the advancing scale of how our needs lie down on the road to satisfaction, inspiration, and the achievement of what we love most. The version of the pyramid (shared by the Doorway Project) you see below displays the five separate layers of needs.

The three stages between the physiological needs and the needs for fulfillment are where marketing relates most explicitly.

- Security

- Belonging

- Estimate

In Maslow's pyramid, definitions of these needs do not necessarily provide a marketing angle for them, so it takes a little creative imagination to see if you can customize your message to suit those needs. Christine Comaford, author and specialist on the topic of persuasion, has found stability, belonging, and confidence to have tremendous importance for our daily work and creative lives: without these three essential keys, an individual cannot succeed, develop, be emotionally engaged, consent or step forward. The more we have (these three keys), the greater the company's success. The greater the partnership, the greater the success of the business.

Her experience has helped her hone three main phrases for power and persuasion and to build a sense of protection, belonging, and matter we all need. They are:

1. "What if." This sentence takes away the ego from the conversation and provides a healthy atmosphere for imagination and brainstorming.

2. "I need your support." This flips the dominant and subordinate positions, includes the other person, and offers a transition of power.

3. "Would it be beneficial if." This sentence moves the emphasis from the problem to the solution.

Here's an example from SEO Nick's Nick Eubanks, who uses the phrase "I Need Your Help" explicitly in an email's subject line. (Come to think of it, one of these three will be interesting to use as an email subject line.)

HOW TO WIN FRIENDS AND INFLUENCE THE AUDIENCE

While you're thinking of manipulating people, our ears perk up at Buffer. Our organizational culture and values are based on a Dale Carnegie book entitled How to Win Friends and Influence People. Christine Comaford's advice above has the famous Carnegie ring to it. Discard the ego. Focus on satisfaction and optimistic mind-set. Be polite to everyone.

A debate on persuasion and power with Carnegie's book could begin and end in a lot of ways. Here's just a section of the book's contents table, packed with ideas about compassion, empathy, and cooperation. (Carnegie would probably hate making you read just the table of contents–he encouraged the readers to read several chapters in his book.) Win people to your way of thinking

1. The only way to get a claim to its maximum is to stop it.

2. Display respect for the views of others. Not say, "You are wrong."

3. If you're wrong, then immediately and emphatically admit it.

4. Start out nice.

5. Get the other person immediately saying, "Yeah, yeah."

6. Let the other person do a lot of the talking.

7. Let the other person believe it's his or her idea.

8. Seek to see things frankly from the point of view of the other guy.

9. Be sympathetic to the thoughts and aspirations of others.

10. The nobler intentions appeal.

11. Dramatize your feelings.

12. Throw a challenge aside.

This is not fantastic stuff?

We try to integrate as many Carnegie values as we can in the way we interact in emails, in articles, and on social media, of course. Below are several Twitter examples of how our Happiness Heroes cultivate friendliness, compassion, and seeing things from another's viewpoint.

For B2B sellers mastering the art of persuasion is about being able to win over others. Don't underestimate the influence of B2B world persuasion. Your target audience may know your industry well, but that doesn't mean they're resistant to sales tactics.

Psychology is all about Persuasion.

Psychology Today's experts have documented how the world's society is evolving and what you need to do to continue to thrive. When you sell to another company, you need to take these measures into account.

Reputation Matters

Business people love referrals and love listening to clout people. Using your credibility to your benefit. Make it clear this is not your first time, and you know what you do. To a lot of companies, it's a feeling of comfort, which is why it always catches their attention.

Place it in Context

You need to personalize your message to make the situation important to the company in which you come in touch. That is where intelligence collection really comes in handy. Make an attempt to grasp the business of the prospect and what they do. Using the experience to present the plan the right way.

Tell a Story

Explain the difference between you and someone else with a story to get the most out of your B2B sales team. A story is also more convincing because it indicates it is not only stating a fact. You see it for yourself rather than anyone telling you this is what happened. You may argue that this brings even more color to the proceedings.

The power of comparison is useful for shifting people from one set of values to another, or selling a product in this case.

Suit the history of the individual Would you like to learn a secret of convincing people? Until approaching them, they read up on the history of the lead. They make an effort to learn as much about them as possible through resources like LinkedIn. Most B2B transactions occurred by linking, based on the fact that the individuals involved went to the same university or studied the same degree. Familiarity gives people a sense of protection and comfort.

Using Friends to Provide an Introduction

Consider plundering your friendship circle if you need to produce any extra lead. Converse with strangers, and see who they meet. The explanation for this is that you already have a good link when you receive a lead from a shared link. Someone is more likely to listen to someone suggested by someone they know and trust, regardless of in which company they are in.

It can take longer to actually hit these leads, but more than make up for that will be the head start you'll have with them.

Get Physical Whether you're trying to win a major sale or convince a lead they need to buy from you, go beyond just words. Sixty-five percent of senior marketing managers said visual aids help tell a story. Consider getting intimate with them by giving them something they can feel and touch. For example, B2B sellers are notorious for showing their lead prototypes while trying to win big contracts, so they can get a better idea of what's being offered.

Get Social Evidence

Your blog is already a monster of the lead generation since it comes with social proof. A successful blog is a motive behind all the social media. It's what you're going to publish so you can draw people into your company. It is an efficient social evidence source, too.

Social evidence will win a deal on Facebook, Twitter, and LinkedIn, also in business circles. Company owners spend the entire day investing as much time on social media as you do.

Solve the problem.

Essentially, making it solve a problem is the best way to convince others to buy what you are offering. You may be as convincing as you want, but if all you do is encourage something, then you won't go far. Businesspeople don't like wasted time. Looking for something they are searching for something that is guaranteed to help them succeed.

Whenever you respond to someone who is asking you about your product, tell them what they can do about it. None of the other stuff.

CHAPTER 5: EMPHATIC COMMUNICATION

THE THREE STAGES OF COMMUNICATION MASTERY

When can you become a Communicator Master? Is it the use of flowery words and the expressions of command? Not exactly. Is it about being descriptive and maintaining a good presence? Obviously, these qualities help, but they are not enough. Master communicators appear to have completed three growth phases successfully, which most of us have not. Here they are:

Step 1: our resumes look incomplete until we gain substantial job experience, and our leadership opportunities, if any, appear to come from extracurricular activities. Of course, we are more inclined to take our bosses back seat at work and let them do most or all of the talking. It is the first level where it all begins.

Step 2: They step up the career ladder over time. We gain more information and use it to develop perspectives and build views on our sectors as they relate to patterns, outlook, policy, and tactics. They express our expertise and thoughts more frequently, both formally (presentations, interviews, panels) and informally (conversations with the mentorship). The more we are conscious of this, the more frequently we continue to talk. But many of us are never going any further than this second point.

Step 3: This most difficult step to achieve includes making sense of highly complex problems in a world where knowledge and consequences are increasing with unparalleled pace and scope, and experience inevitably needs to be more nuanced. There never seems to be sufficient time for us to pass on what we know. A few real master communicators emerge in stage three. They should make it easier without dumbing down. In their central nature, they will distill complicated concepts. We will get audiences of novices to understand, obey, and enjoy complex subjects. They will get people of all maturity levels to ask for more, and take action. They do that by storytelling. By honing your storytelling skills, you will become a master communicator!

All of this sounds pretty interesting, you would think. Yet, based on this chapter, you are a busy person with only limited time to learn storytelling, which seems likely to be very time-consuming! Many of my customers have brought up this exact issue. "It takes time,' I'm telling them. I always tell them there are ways to make the process more efficient— to jump-start. There are five simple business plots, for example, to which everyone can understand and relate. I will explain what these five plots are in the next chapter, and provide you with sketches that will instantly get you to write your tales.

Empathy

People enjoy warm, ups and down colored emotional lives, sweeping highs, and abject lows. The conditions and circumstances which create these moments are special to each person and yet patterned and central to the human condition's life cycles. Yet when life throws something dense and heavy upon us, creating a conglomeration of dark feelings, these can also be crucial times in our lives, leaving us with choices that have real consequences. Moreover, these moments are usually not only ours to bear but can have a ripple effect that affects for good or for bad other relationships in our lives. Some of those moments in my life where the experience I'd just described. It was a turning point where I had to decide what to do with my life while engulfed in a multitude of powerful emotions. But emotions aren't enemies; they actually serve an important role in our lives. As Planalp (1999), one of the leading scholars on emotion, has noted, "feelings are not so much a sign of trouble as a way to keep up the struggle to understand and reconcile an emotionally burdened experience with other convictions about the world and ways of living" (p. 5). Emotions are also invitations to rebuild and realign our experiences with our beliefs, and to direct us to deeper levels of understanding, or to take constructive action. Across these emotions, the task then becomes sifting to find the meaning and course of action that 6 propels us in a positive direction. Ultimately, it was empathy that guided me navigate the dark tunnel that I found myself following my comprehensive tests, it was empathy that gave me some light and clarity, and it was empathy that kept me pursuing the target I set myself years before. My experience isn't special in that. Anyone who has encountered empathy inside a relationship knows how powerful and valuable this can be during stressful or challenging times. It is a sensory experience that can sometimes be difficult to explain, but it can also be unmistakably strong in its creation.

Not only does the force of empathy manifest when major events arise, but its implicit existence also goes unnoticed as it binds us to those around us and to the human race in general. Jeremy Rifkin (2009), in his seminal book, draws on a large amount of research to show how our growing awareness of empathy has gradually begun to transform our perception of the human story. He points out that thinkers, scientists, psychologists, historians, and theologians have always portrayed humans as carnal, greedy, compulsive beings driven by greed and self-interest throughout history. Darwin's and Freud's views have had a profound impact on the scientific world, positing that humans are guided by nature by innate desires and will, therefore, behave egocentrically at the detriment of others. Looking back at history, and the conflicts and violence committed by individuals and organizations, it is easy to see how others could come to such conclusions. Rifkin goes on to point out, however, that there is another understanding of the human experience, one which is now being expanded by neuroscience.

The new theory posits that our lower impulses have not dominated the day as a species, but rather it is our willingness to interact empathetically with each other that has created the nations we see and the continuing search for world peace. We didn't kill each other seven, but over time, as we learned and continue to learn how to co-exist and support one another, the world has become more relational. Scientists have discovered in the last two decades that our brains have mirror neurons, which literally wire us to care about the condition of those around us (Braten & Trevarthen, 2007). Essentially, we are conditioned from birth to care about each other in an empathetic way, and when we nurture this side of our natures, we participate in prosocial ways with others and improve our relationships and our societies.

Empathy, however, performs many roles. As I discovered when talking to my graduate advisor, empathy has the power to turn our challenging and emotional interactions to beneficial ends, and empathy also has the power to connect us with others in ways that promote constructive action that works to enhance our mutual well-being. Based on this, that body of research, scholars, and practitioners have argued that there is a great need to seek a deeper understanding of empathy actively, particularly how it is learned and taught so that relationships and society can reap the benefits of cultivating their strength. The need to educate empathy and cultivate empathy is immanent, from supporting marriages and families to supporting communities and nations. Intercultural scholar Carolyn Calloway-Thomas (2010) reinforced this argument by arguing that, "Empathy is the moral glue that binds civil society together; unless humans have stable mental patterns and reciprocal attitudes that contribute to empathy, society will collapse as we know it" (p. 7). In addition, psychologists and scholars Miller and Striver (1997) promote empathy in these terms: The concept of empathy is central to all our relationships. Either by turning to each other or turning away, we deal with the emotions that are inevitability present in our interactions. If we turn away from others without communicating appreciation of their feelings ' existences, we eventually leave the other eight individuals to some degree diminished. We therefore eventually switch away from completely interacting with our own reality, coping with it in a way that is less than ideal- that is, in isolation. (As quoted in Brown, 2007, p. 57) While the value of empathy has been substantiated in many respects, and its importation is no longer in doubt, there is still significant controversy about how empathy should be described, investigated, and taught. The next chapter will address some of the main issues and complexities associated with this debate. Therefore, it is important to state at this stage that my research project is planned to participate in this debate. In particular, I set out to engage from a communicative perspective in the conversation. As Preston and de Waal (2002) pointed out, "Much of the research on empathy focuses on whether empathy is an emotional or cognitive mechanism, and distinguishes empathy from emotional contagion, compassion, and perspective" (p. 2). Over the last decade, this emphasis has only become more ingrained as scientists have furthered our understanding of mirror neurons and their role in the development of cognitive and affective empathy. There is one dimension of empathy that has been left overlooked and mostly understated as a result of this discussion, and this is the part this communication plays in generating empathy. Empathy as a connective force is more than an inner phenomenon; it is also a communicative one. Some scholars accepted this, positing that "empathy occurs when two separate individuals ' journeys intersect. Empathy occurs where realities intersect, acts as a reference to the other person's facts, and offers insight and comprehension into where one's reality ends and the other begins "(Hickson & Beck, 2008, p. 378). It is this converging communicative dimension of empathy that propelled my interest as a researcher as well as my direction.

And as I was considering what I wanted to do with my dissertation, I realized that there were two important things about 9. First of all, I wanted to do something positive that would contribute to the academic community and its partnership and contact understanding. Second, I knew I wanted to use my research to help people improve their personal lives and relationships. I asked myself this question with these as my guiding concerns: if I want to support people in a meaningful way, what is one aspect that has made a huge difference in my life? The more I considered this matter, the more moments of empathic communication came out of my mind. As I reflected on those times, I knew I would most likely not be where I am today without them, doing what I am doing. Yes, it was the people in my life who got down in the dirt with me, every time I fell on an obstacle (either because of my own actions or circumstances outside my control) and co-created deep and meaningful discussions or empathic relationships with me that made a huge difference in my life. I realized I wanted to research empathy based on this understanding, and this is how I decided to do it.

How will empathy turn you into a stronger communicator?

Okay, you probably already allow empathy to influence your communication patterns very naturally. If we find it consciously or not, we are always being influenced by others who then infer what we say and how we say it. You don't live on an Island, as George Herbert Mead articulates. Each human being lives as what he calls "a social self "— any person is constantly influenced by what the social sphere has handed them over and lives by it. That can be relevant, though, is simply to consider the interconnection with others and to be purposeful about how you want to let your contact affect it. Even others are manipulating you. The further incentive is to act consciously by taking those factors into account and making clear decisions with the others in mind.

Let's say you wake up and get dressed — which is presumably presumed that wearing clothes is common in our culture, something you've been conditioned by (which is also made out of a deliberate revolt against that influence, including the decision not to wear clothes). You may also have a dressing room or bedroom floor full of clothing. And not just any clothes, for the clothing style is generally unique to your cultural standards— we prefer to find just a few out of any possible clothing choice in the world. Some have already inspired whatever you want to wear.

So while you could just throw on anything you want (again, potentially affected by the social sphere), you should also consider who you're going to see or what setting you're going to be in, and what selection of clothing choices would make your expected appearance in certain spaces and social situations easier. To do so, you will not only need to be mindful of social expectations and pressures, but you will also need to understand the people involved's viewpoint and what your clothing choices would convey to them. Do you want to see them as a specialist to you? You want to wear an outfit that culture has found professional (influence) and that you find appealing (empathy) to the persons involved. Do you like to subvert the standards and wear a beanie hat and a hoodie? Okay, you work with a standard (influence) and agree to give a counter-cultural message based on how you believe the people involved view your casual outfit in the light of certain norms (empathy).

All of that and we just covered the shoes.

Notwithstanding our social reality, the inclination toward self-centeredness is profoundly entrenched. Therefore, empathy is a way of pushing yourself to act apart from the norm. You switch from being influenced by others to intentionally dealing with other people's results. You would already be influenced; the act of empathy involves another degree of awareness, deliberate, and measured decision-making.

So, in our specific situations, how does empathy intervene?

Empathy opens you up to better communication, as empathy will take another's viewpoint and think, feel, and behave as you are.

When you connect, you interact with someone else, and you can tailor the conversation to what would be most efficient for the transaction as you enter their minds and see the world from their viewpoint (the empathic process is called, you guessed it, "Viewpoint Taking"). You overcome the automatic impact and make purposeful decisions based on the precise viewpoint of the person with whom you are engaged.

APPLYING EMPATHY IN EVERYTHING YOU DO

I like writing in a story-based style, really. It's a normative choice that's accessible because I was influenced by a culture that made this a popular writing style. There is just something that resonates with me about the stream-of-thought & style of narration. Nonetheless, you will find that this writing is done with headlines and breaks, as well as a written, linear map outlining the details in what might be more intelligible to an audience.

How wouldn't I write the way I like writing?

I think most citizens would prefer the former to the latter. I'm consciously choosing not to necessarily respond to my immediate state and consider what might be better for those reading this. If I want you, dear reader, to consider these ideas that are important to me, beneficial to you, then if I relate and conform with your viewpoint and not just mine, there is a greater likelihood that they will be.

Just being "true to myself?" Maybe. Or maybe this is a compromise. Since I still write in a creative non-fiction style that appeals to my experience but helps me to write on your own. I am trying to reach you in the center because, in my decision-making process, I have to continuously consider your viewpoint.

Often, it's not always the best you want. Often, it is the adapted solution that can bear the anticipated fruit of the contact you expect.

In serving your actual message, the medium can be more relevant.

So first, let's think about what's going on here, and then let's dig into some forms of implementing empathic communication contextually.

The Technical Steps— For Which There Are Two The nuts and bolts guidelines for empathy success (as specified at the end of Part One) are called "Attribution" and "Accommodation." They appear to follow a strict sequential order of attribution first and subsequent accommodation, but this is how you can take the principle of empathy and apply it to concrete action.

Phase One: Attribution The person receiving your contact is given a viewpoint by jumping into their shoes— you take their viewpoint. When you start to see the world from their eyes, you can now make certain attributions on where they are, what they want, and whether they need to obtain something from them. Attribution is the act of gathering information about where your target or recipient is, and how they interpret your message best.

But then, with that knowledge, you still need to do something.

Phase Two: Accommodation

You accommodate what you intend to do, do, or pass on to what you have attributed as the state of your audience or receiver — you adapt your actions & contact to their viewpoint that you have taken into account. Attribution gives you a concrete strategy (putting on the particular clothes depending on the message You want to convey), and accommodation is the act of speaking, behaving, or carrying out the strategy (showing up in that outfit and acting appropriately during the situation).

That's why it's important to have a good vocabulary or scope of your internalized knowledge or experience—because the more words, thoughts, and details you have to work from, the more choices you have to meet the other's communication needs. When they say you're good with words, they may also mean you have a wide toolbox to choose from to be empathetic in attributing and accommodating your communication.

Some Application Instructions A few steps to get you through this process:

1. Contextual Adaptation

You can't just understand any word to make a point, you need to be able to use the strongest, most precise, and tacit word set inside your arsenal that makes the most sense to the other. That is the choice to deal with what the other wants in any given context. You adapt how you want to say by translating the raw meaning in your head into what makes the situation tenser. Too much technological jargon, using words in which your audience has no context, or speaking in a way that only makes sense to you are simple ways to have a communication breakdown— regardless of how reliable or successful the material is. When you use the term you want to use, you are basing yourself on the fact that it makes the same sense to them. But if you can understand their viewpoint, you can choose words carefully which fit into their communicative state. You might argue there are no correct words to use — although certain words could be better— there are only terms that function best in a specific context.

Such intentionality refers to any circumstance in which you express something to another.

You must use language as a parent that makes sense to your kids (even though you want your kids to develop their own language set). When a leader, you have to take into account the experiences, desires, and circumstances of the people you lead. As an organization, you have to deal with your future customers' language collections.

Wherever you're going to talk, say, "What contact do they need? "Depending on your identity and accommodation, make sure to use the response you get to that question— whether it's your preference or not, and whether it's your preference or not. Note that it doesn't mean you have to tell people everything they want to respond to a situation and communicate empathically. Often you have to know where people are so that you can drive them into another future.

That may lead them to declare you're amazing at writing.

Because legally, you are doing this.

You're excellent at tailoring your expressions for your target.

2. Communication is more than words

When placing yourself in the context of your audience and reacting accordingly, it is important to note that communication is not just the words that you use — it is something that transmits a message or knowledge to the receiver.

Therefore, empathically listening is not only about adjusting to what the listener wants to hear but also:

• how they need to hear it,

• where they need to hear it,

• the form they need to hear it in,

• and why they want to hear it first.

You have to ask all these questions and, in answer, anticipate the best-crafted letter.

Empathic communication is not only about changing the language, but it also takes all the factors into account for what happens when you send a message.

For instance, I'm sure you'd like to see this figured out further (an ideal table would be if I weren't lazy because there's some missed empathic communication for you) so here's my attempt to match what I want to say and how I think you'd prefer.

If communication is more than just words, that will mean you have to consider:

• Which words you should use dealing with the receiver's message's lexicon & understanding. How certain words can be placed together from where you bring content and the role it plays in the wider message, to the use of visuals or storytelling, to the sound and style and other non-verbals that accompany your words, to the placement of those words and where they go.

• What the duration is meant to be, which also means you cannot say something you want to say.

• Which channel you use to deliver the message from. This is most important to interpersonal (relationship-based) communication but also applies to the content you may be making.

• What is the sense in which the individual sends the message? His apparent authority, reputation, or voice. You can need to adjust the meaning in order to better respond to the other. In order to clarify the message, you might even need to subvert a preconceived meaning (i.e., a parent giving up their authority to encourage the child. This is called "complementary contact" in reference to authority).

• What will the message's physical or spatial meaning be? The place or time of the message, or its state of being when it is sent.

All this is called "Non-Verbal Communication" and goes beyond words to the communicative process. And as a parent, you need to be mindful of the non-verbals, not just of what you say is correlated with, but also of the non-verbals like proximity and contact and facial expressions and location. And when you're not talking, you need to know what messages you're sending that will connect to your kids.

If communication is more than words, then all you do is say something empathically, it's also extremely important to pass on those messages.

The same can be said for the person leading. You don't just need to be empathetic when you're giving a lecture, running a meeting, or sending an email. The room you make, the manner in which you move in relation to your people, the manner in which you carry yourself, the activities that you do, and engage in, all say something. That's why a company in its advertising or social domain may have majestic language but can cause a lot of problems if they violate an ethical principle that their audience finds essential. If Marshall McLuhan was right, that the medium is the message, then we'll want all of our media to express our messages empathetically, too.

3. Details Are Vital

First, let's agree that your audience can never understand or take into every single word or act of communication. Most likely, you haven't memorized every word written in this post, or even paid attention.

So, you needn't worry about every word, right?

In reality, I would say this is the opposite. Each word, each choice of composition, every single detail must be deliberate. This is why poets are perhaps the best communicators: they work with certain constraints that make every word essential and significant. While not every single word will be captured by the audience, the purposeful craft of every single word generates a flow that the audience will understand. Bad composition, unsuccessful phrases, or confusing material can cause an audience to evaluate the messenger's amateur-ness, which can contribute to the deliberate decision that this message is not worth their time. Also, it would miss the positive messages.

Yet even if they are not completely internalized, clear verbal and non-verbal information has the ability to create transparency and confidence to receive the messages they need to receive. Much like storytelling, you often provide details that aren't the key point, so those details allow the viewer to better grasp the main point even though those details are lost on them after the fact.

Even if every detail may not be appreciated to the same degree that you appreciate it, even if it may not feel worth your time, poring over every detail will build a flow that will decide how the audience determines how to engage everything you make.

So craft like a poet and hold every detail with fragility and care and attention.

4. The Importance of Self-Empathy

This whole idea of being empathic with others can come across as a desire to think about yourself in the course of communication and either play with others to get what you want or give them what they want.

Not so.

We have to understand that if you internalize the belief, it can be very dangerous for other personalities.

• If you're an ego-driven person, you'll be hiding from other people to get what you want, playing various roles constantly to see how they want you to look.

• When you are a personality "helping," you'll sell yourself to make someone else happy.

• You can avoid challenging contact to keep things calm and simple if you're a people-pleasing or peace-making personality.

The empathic cycle will often show that you really have to build a message that is not exactly what your audience needs to hear because it will expose unhealthiness and push them to health. If you forget what you bring to the message or give it up entirely, you lose yourself, and hence, the importance you bring to that phase.

Perhaps we should put it this way— you would only take on another's viewpoint if you first owned your own viewpoint.

Empathy, for another, is just as powerful as your self-empathy.

Basically, if you don't know who you are, what you need, what you need to give, the vocabulary you've learned, or the meaning of what you're bringing to the table— your communication will still be a superficial attempt to please and less effective.

In empathy, you can't lose yourself— empathy will create the most powerful version of yourself in the messages you're making. Call it self-awareness or "knowing yourself," but whether you are a leader or in a relationship, whatever material you communicate must be a precise representation of what's within you, even when it's adapting to the meaning of the other. Only then can you connect and satisfy the audience correctly & healthily.

And just like the poet, don't forget— you're part of the crowd too.

You pour over and word, and you take into account yourself, and even though good content can be created by putting in less effort, you do obtain what you make.

You go through the self-empathy process, as you will always obtain whatever you make, even though it is intended for someone else.

You'll be changed in writing a message. Always keep that in mind.

UNIQUE WAYS TO EXERCISE CONTACT

Public speakers are advised to "know your audience." You have a room full of people, but I believe the group that has been assembled is not a random or impartial collection. Therefore, under the structure of what you know about your audience — the more you can change the correspondence, the more successful the transmission becomes. I might go so far as to advise there's never a generic message or expression that's suited for any crowd. Whatever your message's meaning is — it will need to take form differently depending on where you are and with whom you are.

Along with the application guidelines, here are some communicative issues to ask when generating a message about your audience that you are going to send out publicly:

• Who are they?

• Why are they in it?

• What incentive does it give?

• What are the general cultural or agreed rules (a protest rally would be different from a TedTalk) for the room or event?

• What ideas and vocabulary do they have in common?

• What is it they don't know about?

• How many new ones can you drive in without losing them?

• What amount of attention do they have?

• What photos would be of help?

• Which voice are you going to take on-Authoritative? Pleasant? Storyteller?

- What is human emotional energy in the room? Why do you align yourself with their emotional perspective?

- Which sound of different parts would be better received?

- How do you set up the different pieces of content for delivery? So what the first words will be like? How do you explain different pieces of information, particularly when they are too dense or require jargon? So many parts do you wish to have? How many stories, how many? What badges, ethos, & pathos blend to use?

- How much should you take out (because you can always say less than you would originally want— a general rule is that the audience is less interested in the scope of the content than you are)?

The more empathy you use, the more effective the contact becomes in a large community or public environment.

Writing There are countless ways you can convey what you want to convey — from the meaning of your vocabulary to the structure of your meaning to pictures and graphics that can support your message visually.

What would be the most powerful addition of these factors for your public?

The same public-speaking questions can be applied just as easily to your prose.

That's why many authors resort to clickbait-y titles or tend to sell the seven ideas/secrets/resources to make you productive/happy / better. Since certain writers recognize that people want to be such things, and although I disagree with the use of empathy — the one that uses the viewpoint of someone to get them to do what I want (this is called manipulation, and it takes someone smart and empathetic to manipulate)—it achieves their aim via empathy. It's the same with Mass Media (this is what makes ads so effective— they trick you by selling their stuff from your own perspective).

My main writing advice is this— first, write it down as you need to understand it. Second, write it down so that they can grasp it.

Just think about which particular words to use and how to map your ideas to be better heard by the person at the other end of those words will make your communication more efficient. We should be vigilant about only putting together a piece of writing, depending on what comes to our minds. Some people are able to do so, perhaps because they are already in tune with their audience, instinctively and empathically, and have a great toolbox to draw from. With most of us, we'll only end up replicating what we've been inspired by as "natural writing"— you're using a story here, then a picture, then a table, then a listicle, and so on — and maybe it's not what helps you get your message correctly. Note, there are nonverbal components to write, as well. It is a non-verbal decision just to determine when a sentence ends, or a paragraph begins. Once, alongside words, poetry will lead us through proper compositional imagery.

Make every word, picture, story, emotion, and decision about design, including graphics, a required reflection of your attribution and accommodation.

So, please, don't hijack manipulative empathy. It's nice to make your writing more available to others— to share what you've learned by interacting with where they are— but to use the background of an audience purely for the purpose of building a forum or increasing your leadership or selling anything that isn't just factual, and it isolates you from your readers— it also shows that you're making something out of the box.

Social media Considering your future audience's viewpoint can alter how you make a message. When you just think of how you interact online, we can all say, and we probably won't read what you put out there, either. If you're trying to interact with other people using social media, well, professionally, then you have to communicate with them, not with them.

I don't think I need to say that, but posting your own myopic thoughts on a social media site doesn't usually do much good — it leads to a lot of argument, conflict, and shouting, but it doesn't help much of the people involved, including yourself (except, maybe, a nostalgic feeling of getting your thoughts out and actually being heard). Only journaling, if that is your goal, might be more helpful.

Also important for emphatic social media communication: Each site always has its specific advantages— you shouldn't post on Twitter the same way you post on Facebook or the same way you post on Instagram.

However, the size of the message & the immediacy of the content, its accessibility, and its strategic value are the most important aspects of social media due to the rivalry of the most valuable resources of the user — recognition, attention, and time. Not to mention that social media is built to allow individuals to click — the platform allows people to only give their tools to the content they want. The competition for these limited resources should represent your content.

Meetings I will leave this brief (foreshadowing what kind of empathic contact our meetings will be doing). There is one aspect of sitting down from someone across the table and adjusting the conversation as you go— knowing which questions, facts, or material are most important to the individual(s) present. Such meetings are good, but in corporate and organizational environments, there is another aspect that is usually more important.

Any meeting agenda would represent the perceptions and ideas of those concerned as to how the meeting would work — that both sides turned up with certain material expectations. Sometimes that content is, "We're only going to sit and talk for three hours," but the content has to be accepted through the empathic process, or you're going to end up with frustration, rage, and a disconcerting feeling that our time hasn't been valued.

Empathy is likely to make the meetings shorter, too.

Relationships Empathy can direct your communication, especially with regard to relationships. Could you just put someone across the table and ask: "What's the best way I could say what I want to say so that they understand? "If you're in a disagreement, how are you going to sit (probably next to each other instead of opposite each other)? What tone is it you should have? Facial gestures are you expected to use (nodding, smiling [non-creepily], or imitating their behaviors), and which should you avoid?

Through your relationships, you don't just connect with yourself— the other person's needs should be accounted for. The wonderful thing about empathic contact in an engaged relationship is there's an unspoken understanding that all messages being sent and received always seek the benefit of the other. Therefore, not only will you address all the issues that have already been posed in this writing, you should have particular interests in what this would do to the individual in your presence, and how anything you say or do together will need to adjust to their meaning alongside yours.

Just in general:

- Have you found your contact frequency in accordance with what the other needs are?

- Or the pacing of your comments?

• Or the non-verbals that you communicate while you stand together in the house, and how they affect the other person?

• Or if there are terms that have a specific meaning for that individual that should be used with that common meaning in mind — especially if it causes trauma— because it may greatly hinder communication and make ineffective the aim of connection;

No matter what your aim, all of your communication needs to align with where, the individual is at to be most successful. And if your goal is to piss off the other guy, you also need to consider how they think, feel, and experience the world.

With the people you love, however, particularly if you constantly seek to see, understand, and feel the world as though you are them, how you communicate with that person will constantly change towards the healthiest way to be in a relationship with that person. That again often means saying hard things or causing harm to the on-going relationship.

A LEADERSHIP NOTE

Two important anecdotes from my past: "trust" and "being ahead."

Second, you can't take people where they don't want to go, which means you need to know where they are and direct them to where they need to go (which may be different from where they want to go). When you're trying to lead someone somewhere, you don't just need to know the environment you're trying to lead them into and own the uncharted area for yourself, you do need to adjust to their background in a way the enables them to trust you to take them to what may be unpredictable, strange, or even scary. This starts with you— they have to be sure you know what the fuck you're talking about. Yet they do need to believe that you are related to them, that they are as worried about them as you are, and that the connection is more important than some other purpose or agenda.

Trust is important in leadership, and you are much more likely to create trust if you are in sync with the minds, hearts, and contexts in which you work.

Attributing and accommodating is more important than ever in the Leadership sector because what you have as a leader is just as valuable as the relational equity built up over time.

Second, the meaning of leading folks is that you have to some degree seen and explored the area, and are ahead of them by definition of "leading." But be careful, for there won't be any identifiable shape to pursue if you're too far ahead. You may have seen the planet miles down the road, but maybe they can just take the first step in that direction. Not only do they possibly not want to follow you if you move miles ahead, but they might not even be able to see where you are first.

We always represent imagination as leaders, and we overcome what is natural, and we go in unexplored directions— but the true essence of imagination is empathy; that you can blend your dream with where people are at present.

I found, for me, that empathy causes me to ask, "How did I feel this first? As for me, what was the first step in that direction? "And then my behavior adapts to the experience.

You will be a complete step forward for being motivated to do so. You could be a thousand steps ahead already. Yet empathizing with your culture could mean only staying a half step ahead.

You may need to come back a little bit.

If you are leading something, be in constant harmony with how the environment is viewed, heard, and perceived by the stakeholders, customers, & co-workers.

A FINAL WORD

You may have fantastic content, but if you don't use empathy, if you disregard the recipients of your content, your content will not be relevant to all. There is a risk you won't get an audience.

CHAPTER 6: STORYTELLING IN EVERYDAY SOCIAL LIFE

The art of telling stories is so underrated. And in other things we do in life, it's one of the guiding forces. If you decide to buy something after seeing an ad, for example, which part of it do you think has inspired you? It's the plot, concept, or theme behind it that connects with you more often than not.

When you look closely, then good storytellers are the best authors. Effective story-tellers are the best speakers. What wants to listen on and on to someone who talks without any meaningful anecdote? Okay, when you're paying to listen to someone, you're likely to zone-out within minutes of the lecture.

In your day-to-day life, you will find many moments where storytelling has had a great influence on you.

Let's discuss the numerous situations where storytelling has become a great communication tool:

1. The Best Speakers Are Great Storytellers

Do you note that the best speakers are excellent storytellers, whether they are politicians or lecturers, or the TED speakers? TED Talks are highly common. It brings together prominent world leaders on a forum where they share their experiences to inspire people on diverse issues ranging from education, innovation, and industry to science and creativeness. One of the important factors for TED Talks speakers is their getting interesting stories to tell. It is their art of storytelling that holds the viewer captivated, from their worst loss to their greatest achievement. If it weren't for the brilliant storytelling, then the viewers would probably never return. Who wants an hour's listening to a dull sermon? Storytelling does amazing things.

2. The Best Advertisements are Fantastic Stories

One of the realistic explanations of how advertisements are so important in your life is storytelling. What advertisements do you remember the most? Yeah, the one they'll say a story about. The funny stories and the most painful ones most people recall. That's why India's advertisers use celebratory occasions like Diwali to tell people they need stuff to make important people happy this festive season is in their lives.

3.The Best Writers Outstanding Storytellers

Everyone can be an author. What you need is a good grammar with the words and a way. The thing is not everyone wants to read what you're writing. People like to read and hear tales, even though the Middle East is about war. Recall when the school taught you to write essays and stories. Which did you like better? Most people liked to tell tales. Nobody wants to listen to the papers. Even the news stories are fascinating when there are a clear storyline and a link with the audience.

4. The Best Leaders Are Great Storytellers

When you look at any of the world's prominent leaders, you'll find they've got the knack of interacting with citizens. What is it that makes them connect? What makes them so special? Yeah, they are fantastic storytellers. With tit-bits on events, they can captivate the audience that turns out to be a great inspiration for the audience. They inspire people with stories that communicate with people on various levels, from Bill Gates to the Dalai Lama.

5. The Best Teachers Are Good Storytellers

Asking why do you like some teachers better than others? They could be anyone from your school, your art school, your coaching institute, or any instructor. Healthy teachers know how to remain motivated by learning. They know how to teach the students without the lesson being a boring activity. It is not just the children who like the stories. Anybody likes a great story. There's a fascinating story behind each scientific discovery. When it's shared as a novel, it interacts with the listeners-the students.

6. Parents Need to be good storytellers. Come to think of it; even the art of good storytelling requires good parenting. You may try to teach them a tale about how bad deeds carry bad consequences instead of scolding

the kids for whatever trouble they have done. Kids love stories. Aside from reading the bedtime story, you do for the kids, telling them inspirational stories from your own childhood and life as a parent is vital. The concept behind the storytelling is that it is one of the easiest ways for someone to connect.

Say a story You have it there. Here are a few examples of how, in our everyday life, storytelling has an impact. If you're listening to a podcast in the conference room or your boss, whether it's a good story, you're going to stick with it until the end.

CHAPTER 7: BUSINESS STORYTELLING

Four Types Of Stories You Need In Business

What are your stories? Want various kinds of stories? How many stories do you need to know? How long would it take for these to be found? These are all that questions that I get asked frequently. Various scholars have proposed between six and eight the right number of stories that you need. Stephen Denning, for example, discusses eight styles of stories in The Leader's Guide to Storytelling. Valerie Khoo does the same in Power Stories too. In The Story Dimension, Annette Simmons points out the six types of stories you need to tell in a company, while Christopher Booker explains seven basic stories in The Seven Basic Plots: Why We Tell Stories. (Although Booker apparently worked 34 years on this manuscript, which is a long time for seven stories and my goal is to help you find stories faster than that.

Outlining the four story types

The truth is that there is no right or wrong response to questions about the number or types of stories you need in business. However, I like keeping things easy and productive, so in my experience, I can tell you only need four story types in your Story Wheel business. There are stories of:

1. triumph
2. tragedy
3. tension
4. transition.

A combination of work and non-work related stories would involve all four styles. Let's take a closer look at each form of story, and the various elements inside it.

Triumph stories

These are tales of accomplishment— the moments you're most proud of in your career and personal lives. And it is important to look for a variety of triumphs that are both labor-and non-work-related. Firstly, you'll need to think about what a victory is in your own opinion. Performance looks different to different people and sounds different. In reality, your personal triumphs do not mean you won anything; they do mean you've had the courage to try. For fear of sounding like we're bragging or boasting, many of us may feel uncomfortable at sharing our triumphs at work. Try getting over this. It doesn't have to be about bragging that you got a raise or ran your first marathon to share these types of stories. Reflect on how much the experience actually meant to you, and why the accomplishment was so important. When you show insecurity and modesty, your story should score the right point. Looking for stories that demonstrate how you've helped others succeed is also important. You may have been part of a team winning an award or meeting its annual goals. Or maybe your victory story is about coaching the basketball team for your daughter when they won the grand finale. Or maybe they haven't played a game this year, but they've improved on everyone. Concentrate on how that made you feel. Note, this is about something that looks like achievement or victory for you and doesn't just mean winning. We should always look for reports that indicate that you've been supporting the local community. Did you volunteer through your enterprise? Did you work on a project that did make a difference? Helped with a fundraiser for children, or has a high-rise development stopped in your street? Making a mix of your own triumphs and those that came from helping others or becoming part of a team or group is significant.

Tragedy stories

Such accounts differ from what you find a tragedy to be according to your viewpoint. Some examples will simply be about traumatic events, while others may be regret tales. Stories of regret may be because you have not had the confidence to do so. It could go for a promotion or take the assignment overseas. The regret may be not to ask your life's love out on a date or feel as though you were not spending enough time with your parents when they were older. Many tales of misfortune can be about events that happened to you through no fault of your own. Perhaps the death of a loved one, or the collapse of a corporation that you worked for. However, you will stop sounding like a survivor. Yeah, these things have had a huge effect on your life, but make sure you reflect on what you learned from the experience, instead of simply moaning about the circumstances. You can also think of a tale of disaster which you caused. Perhaps a mistake you made that had disastrous consequences, such as making an error while driving that led to a major accident or giving advice to someone who was wrong in retrospect.

When it comes to sharing tales, realize that you, as the storyteller, are choosing what tales to share with and who to share with. This is the case for all four types of stories, but it is particularly so for those surrounding tragedy because, in particular, these stories can elicit intense emotions that you might not feel comfortable expressing in a working situation. That's all right. This is a call to judgment that you are still in charge of.

Tension stories

Those are conflict stories motivated by your beliefs, your loyalties, or your responsibilities. Stories of stress that undermined your ideals could cause friction because you were forced to choose between two opposing principles. A common example involves a tale about a time when your beliefs weren't being real. Ironically, sharing tales about when you haven't followed one of your beliefs, and the regrets you have for it reveals more integrity than you would expect. For example, if you share a story about how you treated someone with disrespect at work, and how much you regret it, that story reveals that respect is something you highly value. Stories of conflict can also be about a situation where you have been torn between two loyalties. You may have had to choose between two extremely qualified people in your team for a promotion. Perhaps you've gone for a long-deserved break with your kids.

Stories of conflict are also tightly tied to the responsibilities. They can entail a situation where you feel nervous about embracing an awesome job opportunity that would be perfect for your career, but that would mean that your children who have just started in a new school will be unsettled. Look for the everyday routine too — stress will come from having to choose between working late to reach a deadline and going home early so you can prepare as planned. Whoever you are torn to, don't just dwell on the choice you made. Make sure the stories reflect on the inner challenges and the inner or outer stress that the incident created.

Transition Stories

These stories are about important changes in your life. If they relate to work, they may involve events such as changing jobs, companies, industries, or careers. In comparison, non-work-related stories can involve moving nations, divorcing, returning to study, or having children. You don't have to get too hooked about whether the stories are or are not legally marked as work-related. Taking a career break or going back to full-time research, for example, maybe seen as either work-related or non-work-related, depending on how you see it. The most powerful transformation stories take the audience through what you think and felt at the moment. Spending time explaining the pressure you experienced when

Storytelling Skills | 93

making the decision is important, as is detailing your anxieties or anticipation levels. A story that just goes through logistics isn't a tale— well, not a really interesting one anyway. Another thing to look for is changes that may have been imposed on you. For example, being made redundant at work or as a child in moving countries. Your aim is to select a number of different transformation stories, so look for those when you've also selected the shift. Have you had to decide between two separate employers or taking on a position overseas? Have you been deliberating about having babies, moving to the country, or disclosing your sexual orientation? Think also of stories that show when you instigated a transition. You may have agreed to quit, have taken a Sabbatical, or dropped out of college to take a gap year. Unlike the other three-story styles, where daily events such as changing cars or switching from a PC to a Mac can be very strong, it is crucial that you choose transition stories that depend on very significant changes and events. (Whether or not you knew you were going through that at the time.)

STORIES THAT WORK FOR PRESENTATIONS

Did you ever sit through an hour-long PowerPoint presentation of statistics, figures, and numbers that were mind-numbing? Just imagine if it had brought the data to life with an entertaining and engaging story instead. It doesn't matter what kind of presentation you need to give or to whom, the most memorable presenters usually start telling a personal story — just look at, for example, the famous TED talks.

Start well...

A well-crafted and purposeful tale can catch the attention of your audience from the get-go, show off your enthusiasm for the topic you're about to address, and give you instant credibility. Why should you waste your precious opening moments — the time that someone chooses whether to listen to you or continue to check their phone — with impersonal information and targets or with reminders of where the toilets are? The most memorable and engaging discourses or presentations are often those associated with a plot. For example, you can recall when excitement was growing for former president Bill Clinton to take the stage in support of the nomination of his wife Hillary for presidency at the 2016 Democratic National Convention. He walked on the stage and opened with:' I met a girl in the spring of 1971...' Then he went on to tell a very intimate tale of how he met his wife and fell in love with her. This clearly influenced the audience and formed an immediate link not only to Bill but also to Hillary. The speech in that political campaign went down as one of the most unforgettable (although the Clinton loss clearly shows that even storytelling has its limits!).

...And don't stop there

Though stories are a very powerful way to start any presentation, it's just as good to end a story. You don't need to quit using one story, either. Using one big story and linking back to it with many other stories is a more sophisticated strategy, but it's still effective when you pull it off, as Sheryl Sandberg did at the beginning of UC Berkeley in May 2016.

Sandberg is Facebook's Chief Executive Officer and author of Lean In's best-selling novel, and she cited an impressive ten stories in her 25-minute keynote speech at the beginning! From a story about her grandmother, who schooled in Berkeley in the seventies and was her family's first college graduate, to a story about her husband's death. This tragic tale demonstrated bravery and weakness and what she had experienced in times of hardship. While her husband's story was just a few minutes in length, she made many references to it in her speech to carry the messages she wanted to convey to life. Effectively, Sandberg often used humor to lighten what should have been a very somber expression.

During the presentations, the following stories were also shared to communicate, engage, and connect with the audience in a special and unforgettable way. Since it was the day's first speech, it was very important that she set the right atmosphere and mood for subsequent presenters and the rest of the event. In this story, she had a lot to dump, in other words.

Story

I was honored to be invited to host the event today as the women's financial literacy is very close to my heart. As a young girl, I grew up in a single-parent household with a dedicated mum focused on working to meet ends and provide for my older brother and myself. This was during that time in the 1970s when there was no compulsory women's superannuation, and at best, it was random to receive any maintenance payments from the other parent. Mum worked as an elderly professional nursing career, and her income was small, so we lived from pay to pay, and my brother and I had part-time jobs and pocket money to buy the extra stuff we wanted. Mum was lucky enough to get a small inheritance in her 50s, which helped her to buy her own house. This gave her some retirement benefits, as well. Mum retired with a tiny pot of superannuation, but the global financial crash did her best to wipe out a big part of it, so she's now down to retirement and supporting me. I still think of how things would have been different for Mum if she had received any advice on saving early in her life to give her a sense of stability in budgeting a pension. Money matters

Suzanne Smith is MLC's Community Insurance General Manager. The following story about her mum opened a women's and money case and was planned to handle money stress. I don't think she'd ever felt she'd earn enough, or had enough to see someone for financial advice. But we all know the importance of putting away the little bit of successful budgeting in practice. It's a lesson that I am now instituting in my kids as my 15-year-old recently got her first part.

Today we're going to hear from some financial experts who are going to share information about strategies and programs that would have made a big difference for my mum, and that can make a big difference for women who want to know more about financial literacy and are willing to be serious about investing in their own financial accountability.

Outcome

Many women approached Suzanne, also sharing similar stories from their own experiences with their family. She also received an email from the organizers of the event, referencing the story:

Your personal stories about your mother at the beginning really set the tone for the event, and then you pulled it all together to finish by sharing the small but simple and effective strategy you had implemented to give your daughter and son a great start. It was really inspiring and very well received.

As Suzanne articulates,' This reinforced to me the power of stories and has given me stronger confidence to use storytelling to connect and pass messages.'

STORIES THAT EFFECT CHANGE

Some of the greatest problems facing today's companies and leaders are transitions. This may mean an organizational shift or a shift within your team. You may need to get a person to do something differently — to alter their behavior, attitude, or priorities. Regardless of the situation, the issue is that we are still so used to' the way things are' that we dig in our heels and fail to shift or even listen to the point of view of others. In the past, organizational reform has been handled by a very systematic, though the drawn-out process. This process consisted of months of preparation and off-site strategy meetings, accompanied by collaboration meetings designed to improve employee engagement and a comprehensive management and communication plan for stakeholders where structured messages will be circulated through the company through beautifully crafted PowerPoint presentations.

Many claim this never worked. The rapid pace of change in today's world means that our PowerPoint decks are out of date long before they've even been tested for accuracy, and most of our audience usually sleep at the click of the first bullet point slide. It's not unusual to be met with stony silence and disengagement when it comes to convincing others to embrace a change, particularly if the change is linked to a habit they've been doing' forever.' Leaders are now being pushed to convey progress in a more agile and intimate way, cutting through the' noise' and abundance of information that workers struggle with every day. And you can see why storytelling is so crucial to conveying a challenge or transition. Employees these days want fewer data and fewer details and more emotion and a meaningful relation. What does that really mean? How do I feel affected personally? Why would I concern myself with yet another change? How am I supposed to adjust the way I work just because you want me to? A genuine business message story will make the connection more effective than a list of points,' you can do this...' remarks and beautiful images.

Organizational change storytelling In the last decade, I have collaborated extensively with a number of various companies and sectors to support storytelling ability leaders specifically relevant to organizational change. Through this, I identified three main factors for successful storytelling:

1. An organization needs a community that is comfortable with the vulnerability and emotion displayed by its members.

2. An organization needs to invest in storytelling skills for senior executives across the company, as well as skills for key support personnel such as those in public relations and HR.

3. The CEO and senior executive team of the company need to model storytelling as well as story listening.

Christine Corbett, Australia Post's Chief Customer Officer, funds one of the biggest organizational reform programs in corporate Australia (explored in Chapter 13). Christine sees storytelling as a vital part of this change: "When leaders speak in their own words, through a story that means something to them, people remember this story and connect to it, and repeat it over and over. You need to spend the time to get out and speak to your colleagues, and hear their stories, to have this impact. They are the ones who really know what works, and they are going to make a difference.

The ripple effect

Because stories build an emotional bond, we are more likely to recall, understand, and tell other people about them. This causes a ripple effect in an organization, similar to how the grapevine operates, where stories are exchanged through the choice between workers and help break down barriers to action or organizational change. That is important when it comes to any kind of shift driving. You will find several examples of true stories in the next few pages that leaders used to instigate an internal shift, or inspire others to do things better, change behavior, change their attitude, or goals.

Surf's up

Paul Quickenden is the CEO of Putti, a company in New Zealand that offers a low-cost, high-quality platform for quick mobile app and website growth. Paul also needs to remind his global team to keep an eye on the market, so they can easily adjust and adapt. This is the tale he tells with its company divisions and members.

Story

My two eldest children and I were at the beach boogie boarding last summer. I was out in the water with them as the wind was up and helped them catch the waves. Everyone had a wonderful time. We swam between the flags, and there were three lifeguards in action. I had my son out in the breakers at one point, and I wanted to see where my friend, Alex, had been after her last run. I found she had drifted a little along the shore, so I screamed for her to get closer. Then I turned my attention back to the ocean, watching out for my son's next big package. But instead of seeing normal wave patterns, the water was churning up all over. There was something wrong about that. I switched to my daughter but I really looked at her this time. Once in the shallows she was much farther away from me and genuinely trying to get to me. My alarm bells stopped. Right then, my friend, Danny, and I were caught in the same current, plus a 10-year-old girl that was swimming close by. The pace and strength had become something completely different. It was not noticed by Danny and the girl swimming nearby. I looked at the lifeguards, but they hadn't heard that we were in trouble. It was just me, then. I was yelling at Alex to stop trying to get to me and get to the beach. She knew something was up already, and my tone of voice verified it was serious. So she changed her direction, lowered her feet, and got to safety. I kept my baby, who was still goofing around but bound to a boogie board that was floating. The kid was just swimming and got away from us more. She could not close the distance, in spite of her efforts. She started out in fear. It was time to do something dramatic.

So I put my son on top of his boogie board and told him he'd never been using an iPad again if he let go. He knew this was serious now. Then I let him go and made my way towards the girl. I grabbed her, pulled her to my friend, grabbed him, pulled both of them to the sea. Averted Situation. It was a situation which has never been for most people, including the lifeguards. They had clearly not known it. The people who ought to have seen it asked, "What happened?The reason I share that with you is because it reminds me of the market in which we are playing. Conditions can shift within a blink of an eye and if we don't see them, we may be left on the sidelines wondering what happened.

Outcome

The story's personal dimension did work. People were interacting with it far deeper than I expected they should. It's the same message every strategy book or consultancy pedals, "Paul says," but the story seemed to have more impact. Paul also comments that many people use the usual sporting analogies in the form of pressure management, but this tale is special and has a much greater effect.

TELLING STORIES WITH DATA

BIG DATA IS EVERYWHERE. Only the fastest scanning of online business news can generate a torrent of stories on what corporations are trying to do with large, often creative data sets. For example, human resource management and payroll company Automated Data Processing has tested software that could allegedly predict the probability of future workers leaving based on their salary, commute distance, and a variety of other factors.[1] Clear Channel Outdoor, the nation's largest billboard company, has generated billboards that can be customized to driver preferences based on data collection. Political campaigns, including retailers, have used Big Data to formulate and communicate key messages to target voters, particularly for the 2016 presidential election. As noted in a 2016 Forbes report, "Info breadth means that any message released, whether it appears on the internet, in a voice, in an email or by canvassing, can be anything better than one-size-fits-all."[3] Big Data also has agricultural applications, as modern software systems can use sensor-based information to help farmers identify the best strategies— such as seed location — for optimal usage.

In short, we are in a time of Information Mania, with nearly every public and private sector experiencing unparalleled knowledge and information-analysis resources available. If you're a data scientist, marketing officer, policymaker, or research analyst, the increasing scale, pace, and data variety4 poses one crucial question: how do you convey to your audience the significance and implications of vast amounts of relevant information, get it on board with your ideas and plans?

The response to that is simple: story. The use of key storytelling elements will significantly improve the impact of your message and prevent you and your audience from drowning in an ever-increasing sea of knowledge. This chapter is about how to use the story to most efficiently convey data-rich messages, starting with knowing the audiences and what matters most to them.

The Number One Problem: Too Much Information

My family and I moved into a bigger house four years ago. Although the change was welcome, it also required a multitude of improvements to the bathroom and kitchen, installing window treatments and cabinets, repainting, etc. The good news was I had the help of a skillful interior designer. The bad news was that we were struggling to reach out. I would inquire about prices or delivery dates — for example for bedroom curtains — and instead of replying directly to me, she would provide a wealth of details that seemed irrelevant: "I went to the supplier's' working room' and asked about the popularity and available fabric yard and they said. And then, three times, I spoke to the seamstress, and she said. .".. I'd get my answer occasionally at the end of the monologue. I wouldn't, sometimes.

When I thought more about it, I realized that with lots of service providers, from auto mechanics to IT support workers, this sort of contact problem happened. Only recently, when I talked to Greg Kim, a friend who handles customer retention for a big online retailer, manages a team of data scientists, I got a better perspective on this trend. "Why do they do this, you know, right? "When I discussed my annoyance with verbose service provider explanations, he said. I went so far as to suggest that some of them may have been motivated by money because they were paying by the hour. "No," he said, "they're doing it to prove their value." That is, they want me to know how hard they've worked, how professional they are, and how they've bent backward to provide me with service. On the other hand, I just wanted a simple, succinct answer to my question, with the chance to ask questions if necessary.

Seeing the gap helped me appreciate the difficulty of making a data-based presentation: the presenters want to show exactly how much data they have gathered — increasing not just their own importance and credibility, but also the importance and credibility of the information they provide. Nonetheless, a flood of data doesn't impress the viewer. We want to know what the data is and why they should think about it.

Data Plus Story: A Modern Leadership Model

In October 2015, I had the privilege of conducting a workshop on how the Advertising Research Foundation would produce captivating presentations. On a break, the organization's executive VP, Michael Heitner, shared with me a casual comment that eventually helped lay the groundwork for this chapter. Heitner said he found that many professionals are concerned about working on their projects and planning relevant presentations so that they are really tired by the end of the day. We are, in reality, so exhausted that sometimes they even forget they still have to give the actual presentation! All that takes part in the planning prevents them from attending the presentation adequately.

Indeed, the more we are absorbed in a subject, the more we become knowledgeable, and the more we can lose contact with the audience in question. "Curse of knowledge" is the idea that if we know something, it's almost difficult for us to imagine what it's like without understanding it— in other words, putting ourselves in the shoes or seats of our audience becomes a lot more daunting.

Successful data communication includes achieving for ourselves (as presenters) and our audiences six main milestones:

1. We conduct data analytics. This is also the stage with the most time. So all-consuming, in fact, are five other steps involved to those in charge of recommending actions and decisions to their superiors that they forget there! And the other five steps (below) all apply to telling good stories.

2. We need to know the analytics. Nowadays, many highly skilled experts have to interact with non-technical peers. For example, an insurance actuary will clarify how she has made pricing decisions for rates for different goods to the consumer representatives, underwriters, and managers of her company. An oncologist must advise patients and fellow medical practitioners on the risks and benefits of various care methods. Non-technical viewers still don't grasp the information relevant to analytics, so they won't speak up or ask for clarity, whether due to ignorance or embarrassment. Regardless of the cause, a whole lot of time and energy is wasted when the audience doesn't really grasp what you're trying to say at a basic level. We do not see your interest in these situations either, so the goal is to ensure clear understanding as a base.

3. We pass on perspectives and consequences. Data analytics can be very fascinating, to be sure. But don't forget analytics are merely a means to an end. (Sorry, data scientists!) The main aim of conducting data analytics in most settings is to provide leadership with fresh, key insights to make the most informed decision with the tools available. The main aim, as such, is to extrapolate those observations and make them perfectly evident in your interactions early on.

4. We (hopefully) approve of us. Also, if your audience completely understands your analytics, they may agree with your observations, or may not. Have you ever worked with someone who studied the same data collection as you but ended up with an entirely opposite conclusion to yours? Ironically, when the

observations you produce contradict the values of your followers, something powerful instantly and subtly bolsters their hardened convictions. When resistance is built inside us, a breakup will not be possible. And yet there's a way out there where there is a will. I'll show you exactly how!

5. We convince them to act and control them. Data initiatives answer two key sets of questions: a. What is going on, or what was going on?

a. What happens well for us? If so, how do we make sure that we completely draw on that? If not, what will we do to safeguard ourselves?

It is difficult to convince audiences in the sense of those two issues. Inertia is widespread. Reform is complicated, and customs are incredibly difficult to kill. This produces norms, establishes expectations, and directs behavior, once organizational dogma is created. So it is especially difficult to take behavior that goes against norms and beliefs. In this situation, how can you trigger change? That's what this chapter is all about, and I'm going to offer practical tips in the next pages.

6. They approve of the action we suggest. Leadership is about fostering both the short-and the long-term positive shift. We need us to take steps to do so. Everyone likes to hear a story. But then what happens? The best stories about leadership promote, direct, and take prompt action. Let's talk about how those stories can be made.

The model provides a structure for the process and ideal outcomes of presentations based on data. The next step, though, is realizing how we can do it now that we know what we want to do. The first step is to get to know the audience. As seen in the next segment, you should communicate the details so that they can understand the information if you know your audience.

Of course, the ultimate aim of your presentation is practice, not just speaking. That's why once you know your audience, you'll want to use the storytelling elements and strategies to convey perspectives and consequences, and also to convince and influence action. In this chapter's final part, I'll cover how to weave data and story into a convincing and inspiring presentation.

Know Your Audience: The Five Areas

A poor understanding of the makeup and desires of the audience is why so many data-rich presentations do not have adequate responses, observations, or takeaways. As noted above, there is always a difference in what presenters find share-worthy and what the audience would like to hear. Kimberly Silk, a data librarian at the University of Toronto, emphasizes this point: "The difficulty of using data to support evidence-based decision-making is that while we collect a lot of data and have a lot of responses, we are still guilty of not answering the question [which matters most to the audience]."[5] Going back to my earlier story, if you put yourself in the contractor's shoes, it's just that. But from the point of view of consumers, the quicker the responses they need are delivered, the quicker they will get on with life, and the more value-added their contractors can become.

Then what to do?

The response goes back to the listener: It is key to good communication to consider the listener. Understanding your audience is particularly crucial in environments with large amounts of data that can be communicated. There are five groups in which an audience may fall, according to a Harvard Business Review article:6 Intelligent Outsiders. These are people who have no prior exposure to your field of expertise or in-depth experience in data analytics. Nonetheless, they are insightful and are always well-educated and demanding members of the audience who are both familiar with the industry and who do not appreciate dumbing up content. Financial advisors, for example, sit through new product presentations from wealth management firms. Although they have gone through comprehensive training and passed stringent licensing exams, they are not fund managers, they are not portfolio managers, and they do not understand the complex valuation processes that fund-management companies use to curate investment goods.

High-level Cross-functional colleagues These are the "A-Team" of your company, colleagues from marketing, logistics, finance, accounting, sales, human resources, and other fields who are familiar with your topic and seek a more detailed understanding and, in particular, knowledge of how your topic could affect their areas.

As in the Game, he is your direct boss, the person who not only respects your work but also stands by it. It is the person who will forward your suggestions to higher-ups as if they came from her. In short, based on your job, the boss might well be taking a gamble on her future. Therefore, she would like to provide "in-depth, actionable knowledge of intricacies and interrelationships with access to detail."The managers in your manager's headcheese(s) or people sitting in your company much higher up. These managers are constantly busy, with no time or patience. They enjoy the conciseness and sometimes need it. Most presenters may not understand the number of important decisions that Head Cheese has to make on a daily basis, and therefore may be shocked to learn that high-level executives do not know or recall why somebody is first presenting on a given subject.

Fellow experts It is likely, particularly in academia, think tanks or research organizations, that those in the seats of the audience are fellow experts who know just as much about your subject as you do, if not more. In this case, clarification takes a back seat, especially in the context of storytelling. Rather, this audience would prefer to examine your methodologies and performance and even criticize them.

Here, we believe that you, the writers, are the data experts irrespective of the type of audience. You can not even call yourself data scientists. Nonetheless, your job is to collect, process, evaluate, interpret, and present data so that you can help your audiences make the most informed and insightful decisions accordingly.

Understanding which form of audience you interact with –based on the above categories–is the first step towards enhancing data-rich communications. The head cheese will require a very different presentation than would be the case with Knowledgeable Outsiders. If you have a better grip on the structure and desires of your audience, you can transition to using "data storytelling" to convey your message.

A Five-Step Method To Link Data And Story

Mastering the following steps and skillsets is needed to become an effective data storyteller.

1. Practice Empathy: Put yourself in the shoes of the public.

2. Prove and Convince: Know when to do what.

3. Words Over Numbers: highlight terms to ensure that numbers are kept.

4. Creating Meaning: Define and emphasize the "so what."5. Show them what they want, tell them what they need: concentrate on what they need to hear from your audience.

STEP 1: Exercise Empathy

I'm thinking about perspective and how important it was to put yourself in your audience's shoes. It is especially relevant for data-based presentations because it is easy to get hit by the Curse of Knowledge:

once we learn something, it's almost difficult for us to imagine what it's like not knowing — that is, putting ourselves in the shoes of our audience. Once you open PowerPoint and launch through what you think your audience wants to know, do the greatest favor to yourself and anyone else by answering three presentation-prep questions.

Three Questions to Plan. Spend time answering these three questions— on your own and with your team— to save substantial time and energy down the road. When you sharpen your message and better understand the needs of your audience, you also have the opportunity to go back and refine responses to those questions.

1. How is my audience's makeup? Why is it they have to know? (Use the five main audience categories mentioned earlier)

2. I hope my audience can recall the following points after listening to my talk, even if they can't remember something else I say to them: (up to three key points articulated in 10 or fewer words each)

3. What are the most important issues facing my audiences at the moment outside of the project I am speaking with them about? Why is it that keeps them up at night?

The answers to these three questions will serve as your guideposts and will inform your communication structure and content. Additionally, the answers will serve as filters to help you remove and sharpen your presentation from outside data.

For example, I worked with a young client at an online travel company several years ago, who was a successful business-intelligence analyst. He had spent weeks studying and then planning for a presentation on business growth. His job was to address the question of whether his company would grow into a particular foreign market. He was already looking at close to fifty pages of data filled slides after going through three drafts of the PowerPoint presentation. Since he had invested so much time and energy on the project, he felt like he couldn't say what was and what wasn't important anymore. And I told him to go through the Three Questions on Prep. Here's a paraphrased version of his responses.

1. My main target is our planning department, Senior Director. He will make more suggestions to the parent company's CEO after listening to my presentation. He'll also be asking a few people in the planning department to listen in. Yet the Main Audience is the Chairman.

2. If my senior manager from my presentation doesn't remember anything else, I sure hope he will remember that:

a. Ease of use (website) is important no matter what market and product. [12 Phrases. My client has been through two terms. I cut him some slack as he had just two must-remembers.]

b. It can immediately expand into the target market.

3. 7 Words. Why is it that keeps this guy up at night? He is still fairly new in the sector. I heard an

unconfirmed report that he did not willingly quit his last employment and that he was actually terminated. Why else would he take this job a step back in his career? Not just for the online trading affection! Nevertheless, he wants to try to prove himself. He'll probably quiz me on how my suggestions come up. Come to think about it, not only does my argument need to be backed up by evidence 110 percent, but I do need to think about how to phrase the whole thing, so it will make him seem like a thought leader, and he can help us gain a major advantage over our competitors.

My client created a conceptual filter in the course of answering these three questions and began to look at his fifty slides differently. He was extremely selective about only the details that would help him advance his goals, instead of seeing anything as significant. He still had ready to share all his data and models, but they were no longer part of the main presentation. Finally, he trimmed the presentation down from almost fifty slides to seventeen.

STEP 2: Prove and Persuade

We were educated to back up our responses during our formal education. "Show your work," the math teachers told us at every level of education. Indeed, if we failed to demonstrate the measures we had taken to arrive at the answers, we would earn only partial credit on exams, if any, at all, even for correct replies. And we are conditioned to "prove" our answers and ideas.

The problem is that, in an academic setting, the laws of the professional arena vary from expectations. Many of us fail to know that, in part because no one has specifically taught us that successful communication in a data-rich environment requires an understanding of the difference between proving and persuading.

What's the difference between convincing and proof? Proving is collecting the best empirical processes and facts. Conversely, persuading your target group is getting them to agree with your point of view and take action accordingly. Typical scientific journals like Nature or the New England Journal of Medicine are good examples of evidence. Within these publications, you can read papers that are written in very technical terms that provide research literature reviews, theories, mathematical formulas, process writing ups, findings, and conclusions. To order to achieve wide approval for their theories, scientists and other researchers must demonstrate the rigor of their experiments, challenge the weaknesses of their own studies and encourage further research to substantiate their experiments. On the other side, a candidate in a campaign speech persuades and attracts supporters by carefully designed correspondence using deceptive phrases and limited information to arouse emotion and support.

You need to have material of both kinds when writing stories in data-heavy environments: demonstrating and persuading. But, as discussed above, you have to understand the difference between the two forms, and know when to use each. Many of the practitioners are well qualified to prove points and assumptions based on their academic experience. Therefore, an effective supplement would be the inclusion of compelling material that emphasizes words over numbers and a tendency to express the "so what."

STEP 3: Words Over Numbers

The title suggests that words are more important than numbers, and should, therefore, be compared to numbers. This approach also underlines the critical essence of numbers. How? How?

No matter how strong our potential for memory has its limits. The truth refers to the amount of numbers that we can keep inside our brains. Psychologist George Miller, who published the paper "The Magical Number Seven, Plus or minus two, "10 developed in the mid-1950s what became the commonly accepted notion that an average person may keep only 7±2 numbers in his working memory. Since there is insufficient space to store numbers, we have to be very selective about how many numbers we give our audiences.

STEP 4: Build Meaning

"Data does not make sense. We do, "says Susan Etlinger, a market analyst with Altimeter Group, where she focuses on data and analytics.13 In 2014, she made a pointed statement in front of her TED Talk audience that, in the Big Data age, we are potentially more in danger of making the wrong decisions based on results. Yes, the opportunity arises with access to Big Data to act upon what we believe we know. As such, the role of data storytellers is not just to ensure their audience understands their interpretation and agrees with it. They must also focus their research on creating decision-making implications.

Importantly, data storytellers and decision-makers are not always the same person. For other instances, the ultimate decision-maker sits in the company at a higher level and spends much of their valuable time listening to presenters like you, finding analyses and feedback as a basis for their decisions. Therefore, you are also making meaning for them if you promote this cycle well. Why do you offer to mean?

Simon Sinek, author of the book: Starts With Why gives a clear yet powerful answer.14 In general, almost all we encounter in these days can be divided into three categories: Why, How and What. Everybody knows what his or her work is, for example. Few know how to get the job done. But, very few people know why they are doing what they are doing. Interestingly, that motivates the cause. Focus on the whys and whats of the content you're providing to build meaning for decision-makers. So if decision-makers are suspicious of your results or eager to find out more, they'll wonder how you've come to your conclusions.

GIVING YOUR STORY A FINAL TEST

Give it a short drive once you've crafted your story before you take it out on the road. Tell a friend or colleague about your experience, and ask them the following questions: What details do you recall from my experience? This question is relevant because most of us get inundated with daily knowledge. It is tempting to incorporate as much data as possible into our response. But then, what good would it do if you don't know what you've just shared with them? On the other hand, people sometimes remember the most random details. And there's no way to find out but to go straight to the outlets and find out what's sticking with them, and what isn't. You're much more educated and prepared to refine your stories after you've gathered the reviews so people know the pieces you want them to know.

How does that make you feel about my story? Remember the advice from Maya Angelou, "people can never forget how you make them feel."5 How did your story make people feel? The emotion evoked is likely to have a much longer-lasting effect on your audience than anything that you actually said. Will a member of your test audience feel inspired? The story may be reminded her of her own experience? Would your colleague or friend feel puzzled after your test run? He may have already begun to look at his watch and wonder when the talk with you is over. Or, is your fellow Member curious? Maybe he can't wait to follow up on the questions that inspired your story. In reality, encouraging your audience to ask questions is an ideal place to start a conversation about the post-story, whether in a formal job interview or casual networking session. As stated in the next bullet, you can ask for this directly.

Having listened to my story, what are your questions for me? That is the target we should all be aiming at: to empower our audience with the right questions. Your story's first or second draft may not have prompted a lot of questions. But shaping it to the point where the audience starts asking questions is a sure sign you are on the right track. When you get your audience to think more about who you are, it's time to look at how the kinds of questions you asked to contribute to the kind of topics you're hoping to address after the initial discussion. For example, after hearing Kelly's story, potential clients might want to know, "What are some examples of times you've brought to a business issue the curiosity of a journalist and the creativity of an Eagle Scout?" Or " This is an ongoing question that we are looking for someone to solve— can you tell us how you will do that?" The stories mentioned in the examples section above lead the proverbial horse — in this case, the audience— to water, but they don't push the horse into drinking. They do not set out five points that tell listeners why they should contract, recruit them, or invest in their idea. Instead, the tellers have told their stories to persuade and manipulate, with a strong underlying sense of whether they want their stories to be taken away from the audience.

And while stories aren't the same as arguments, to convince you always say your story. But, based on the input from your colleagues, refine your story until it conveys the exact message you want to express, as shown by their reactions to the story and related questions.

You now have all the resources you need to build an engaging and compelling narrative when someone has taken an interest in you and asks you the question, "Tell Me About Yourself." But, what happens when anyone actually cares for you and asks you to say something about yourself? Although "tell-me-about-yourself" may not be your favorite issue, "what-do-you-do" maybe even more demanding. Yet most people should have something smart about that at networking events. Alas, most are not.

CONCLUSION

People have always told stories, and they're a crucial part of our daily communication, but stories have meaning beyond the importance of entertainment. In reality, storytelling is a great business skill and can improve a company in a variety of ways if successfully applied, such as enhancing consumer loyalty, developing a good marketing strategy, increasing income, and so on.

Stories lasted as long as there were people. Stories make up our past and direct our future from the stories told in paintings on the ancient caves at Lascaux (Google it!), to the bedtime stories told to young children.

Every day you're surrounded by stories. Articles on TV, radio, and in the newspaper are nothing but myths. The Bible is full of myths, among many religious texts. Many stories are the lessons teachers offer in school. Songs are about myths. The pictures tell stories. Films tell tales. Comedians are incorporating stories into their routines. When you tell a friend, you are sharing a story about something that happened to you. Can you imagine the last story you have heard? Think hard: Maybe you heard it just a few minutes ago!

Some tales have been going on for hundreds and even thousands of years, and are being published. Stories originated with the oral tradition, meaning they were passed on by listening and retold. People later started writing down the stories, but we really enjoy hearing stories told out loud.

Stories are solid. They can teach morals— the ideals which the story author believes people should live by. They will do history teaching. They should have us amused. They can make us think about things in ways that we have never before thought about. We will make a joke on us. Might make us sad. Telling stories is a huge part of what makes people bond.

Stories are an important part of any society. Stories of our country and its history enable us to feel proud of our country. Stories of our ancestors tell us where we come from, and what we have in common with those around us.

One of the most important topics in content marketing today is the company storytelling or corporate storytelling, as most people refer to this term. It's what consumers and fans demand from us marketers, and it's all about delivering the right message at the right time at the same time.

Let's face it: Marketing myths.

They can communicate easily with them, and at the same time, understand them. What about Corporate Business? Can you make storytelling part of your marketing strategy? Is storytelling about companies really a thing? What is it all about, and how can you integrate this idea into your own strategy? Okay, let's seek to answer one by one to these questions—storytelling company. The definition I think it's important to define our key terms of this article and understand their significance before diving into the subject. So let's start by asking and answering the most important question that comes up at this point: What is the storytelling of corporations?

I don't think there was a period in human history when people didn't like telling stories, sharing stories, and listening. Stories are an integral part of our lives, and they have also become very relevant in marketing lately. A corporation, whether small or corporate, isn't just a company anymore. It needs to tell its own story to grab the customer's attention, and it needs to do it as well as humanly possible.

As a result, corporate storytelling is about telling/presenting the brand to the public using narrative methods in a story-like narration. It is essentially a communication strategy that ideally lures the brand's readers by expressing their ideas in a creative and insightful manner.

In conclusion, storytelling and corporate storytelling allow you to communicate through stories in a simple and attractive way. It is the native way people communicate, and this also makes it efficient for communication-related to marketing.

Where does storytelling work at the company? What makes this communication technique so different, and how does it work? Okay, the best I can în the following few pages, I'll try to answer certain questions.

For our species, storytelling is the normal form of communication. Stories may change, and the ways of telling stories may change and evolve, but there will always be the consistency of narrative: people will always have stories to tell. Stories promote our contact, the way we understand each other, and help us communicate more directly and easily.

You want people to connect with you as a brand, emotionally as well as commercially. And, stories virtually immediately cause emotions. They make our lives meaningful and help us communicate information, pass on knowledge, and consider our history, present, and future.

That's how storytelling works, and that's how storytelling even works. The idea is the same, only the means to an end are different from telling of a brand versus telling a story about your last trip to Paris.

The more you're explaining it, the easier it is for you to communicate with the viewer and win their ears and minds, making them pay attention to what you're doing.

The added benefit of a corporate storytelling marketing strategy Corporate storytelling advertising is something that is particularly important about how the viewer makes the first contact with your brand and then their first new interaction with any of your goods, services, and promotions.

They all begin with an idea and then the battle that transforms it from a dream or concept to reality. Within that story, the heart, the essence of your brand or product is captured, which can be brought to life through storytelling. This technique transcends the conventional approach and allows you to share the knowledge in a manner that is easier for the public to understand and relate to.

Storytelling avoids the conventional call to action as opposed to other forms of marketing and advertisement strategies. Some of these techniques include these CTAs, but most of the time, they are subliminal, dressed in a different style that is more normal and thus similar to the way people speak and relate their stories naturally.

However, the call to action is the story itself, which can have greater and more consistent results than conventional approaches.

Why use ads for storytelling?

Ok, I think I've addressed this question already, but I still feel the need to emphasize the basics. Let's make a short and detailed list of all the benefits we've spoken about so far, in detail: Corporate storytelling helps you to communicate a message relevant to marketing in a new and personal way that the viewer can appreciate and relate to.

Through a more realistic way, corporate storytelling sells the brand by interacting without the rigidity of conventional marketing and more like how people interact with one another.

Since corporate storytelling is a natural mode of communication, it can activate confidence and more public interaction, as well as an enhanced awareness of the brand across media outlets.

Storytelling is also capable of cultivating consumer engagement as long as the story is successful, and it can affect the public.

Company storytelling is about linking people to the brand, a product, or a campaign.

Is there a recipe for a strong approach to corporate storytelling?

Of course, each story will be told differently depending on who's telling it, who's approaching the storyteller, and with what expectations.

I can't teach you how to compose a good narrative, but I can also describe some of the best approaches and choices you need to explore to make the most of your corporate storytelling approaches.

I will also give you some very good examples of business storytelling that will shed some light on what this kind of content is, and why it has more effect on the viewer than other styles.

A. The tone of voice This part is very critical because when you tell the story of the brand, you have to adapt the approach to an audience-based narrative and the tone of voice of the brand. And, when I say consumer, I'm referring to the segment that you're talking about. Who are they, then? How old are they then? What social category will they better fit in?

It's important to answer these questions first because the sound of the voice is obviously different when you're addressing teens, IT professionals, senior citizens, etc. Finally, you need to find the perfect formula for your brand, a formula that never changes even if the message changes based on the current campaign.

The story style and the features that make it successful If you stop thinking about your campaign and the audience for a few seconds, these are the most important features of a good brand storytelling strategy: A good story is simple. It's easy to understand, easy to read, easy to respond to, and able to express the message in a straightforward way without making it more complicated. You need to express a key message, and nothing more.

Complete of a good story. Only look at stories from Facebook or Instagram. You see them slide by slide, but you foresee a closure in the end. You want it to stop. Will you come back and see someone who doesn't give a resolution for more stories? I do doubt that. Each narrative requires a conceptual structure, be it a visual narrative or a written material of a long length. This logical structure means a beginning, an end, and a center.

There are a few great examples of corporate storytelling I can pick from here, both easy and total. Nonetheless, I will use only one as a guide, the case of Hinge, a dating app that was introduced as a rival for Tinder a few years ago.

Their campaign used a lot of consumer data and real personal stories to illustrate the advantages of moving to their services, as well as the problems people experience while looking for a partner.

A good story travels. Yeah, you really need to get to the audience, cause some emotions, make them feel something to send an effective message. A strong storyteller knows how to tell a story in a way that grips and stuns viewers. But pay attention to what kind of emotions you want to evoke because your story depends on them for its effectiveness. Will it be happiness? Dumbness? Melancholy, right? How then do you want them to feel?

And yes, you can also find a lot of examples of business storytelling for this. Here's one of my favorites, a perfect example of a moving story Google was making and sharing as a digital video ad.

It tells the story of an old Indian man who reconnects with his granddaughter's childhood friend via Google Search to track down. A true and real good story. So here we are talking about ads, truth is always important. Your story should be genuine and reflect your brand, product, or service's true story, as well as telling the audience what added value they will derive from that. Also, keep in mind that you can interpret everything you say as a promise, and you will have to keep that promise to validate your words or messages.

That is a good story. As I have said before, you need to add value to the audience and not just say an empty story in order to make your efforts successful. One of the most important aspects contributing to this importance is significance. It means you have to share a story that's also tailored to the audience and not just the brand that you're marketing with that story. In summary, ensure the narrative resonates with the audience. Otherwise, the impact will be little to no.

Marketers still strive to make their content meaningful to the target market, and that's why you'll find plenty of examples of business storytelling and examples of corporate storytelling to apply for this term.

That's a good example of clear fact-based storytelling material. A good story has to have meaning, characters, and action. These are the same criteria for any other form a story requires, and not just one relevant to marketing. A context refers to a particular time, place, or condition, often all of these three variables combined. The characters are important to the action as the action adds salt and pepper to each story's interesting part. There's no story when nothing happens, anyway.

The story's Hero. As you may already know from books, movies, and other such information sources, every story is based around a central figure, the narrative hero. The quintessential character is the one that reflects the positive characteristics that activate the audience's positive emotions, and in this case, that character should be the brand or product you are selling. The hero in traditional stories is typically the one people are sympathetic to. The hero gives life to the story and makes the viewer want to be part of the story. Therefore, creating this type of character is critical, and building everything around them.

Business or corporate storytelling, as most of us use the term if you use it wisely, is a powerful device. The narrative is a perfect marketing approach, and with this technique, a lot of businesses and organizations have already tried and succeeded.

You may not be a pioneer in this area; therefore, but at the same time,, you can learn a great deal from their experiences and knowledge from the outset that the approach works.

Ever use storytelling as a tactic, and if so, what are your results?

Thank you for reading this book. If you enjoyed it, please visit the site where you purchased it and write a brief review. your feedback is important to me and will help other readers decide whether to read the book too. Thank you

Printed in Great Britain
by Amazon